EMPTY PROMISES

EMPTY PROMISES

Quality of Working Life Programs and the Labor Movement

Donald M. Wells

Foreword by Staughton Lynd

Monthly Review Press
New York

Library of Congress Cataloging-in-Publication Data

Wells, Donald M., 1946–
  Empty promises.

  Bibliography: p.
  1. Quality of work life—United States.   2. Trade-
unions—United States—Officials and employees.
3. Quality of work life.   I. Title.
HD6957.U6W34 1987   331.25   87-24687
ISBN 0-85345-710-7
ISBN 0-85345-711-5 (pbk.)

Monthly Review Press
122 West 27th Street
New York, N.Y. 10001

Manufactured in the United States of America

10 9 8 7 6 5 4 3 2 1

For my father, John Page Wells, Jr.

Contents

Foreword • Staughton Lynd

Workers I know who have experienced Quality of Working Life (QWL or Labor Management Participation, or whatever name it goes by) typically have two reactions. On the one hand, they are flattered, stimulated, and excited by the opportunity to make—often for the first time in their working lives—suggestions, use their imaginations, solve problems for themselves, and work without a foreman looking over their shoulders. Most workers want to make a quality product. QWL appears to give them that opportunity.

On the other hand, workers deeply resent the trivial character of the decisions to which this opportunity is confined and the manipulated nature of the process as a whole. This is especially so with respect to decisions about plant shutdowns and capital flight. It is a painful irony that capitalism should offer workers the chance to participate in decisions about the mini-environment of their immediate work setting at the very moment when, in communities across the face of North America, it destroys entire enterprises by macro-decisions about where to invest capital so as to maximize profit.

A friend who works on the assembly line at the General Motors plant in Lordstown, Ohio, has a theory to account for this two-sided reality that he experiences. He works in a group that has no foreman, and he and his buddies plan the work for themselves. Soon they will no longer be required to punch in and out. What this is all about, according to my friend, is that the bosses are positioning themselves so that when they close the plant, they can blame the workers for it. "They'll say it was our fault," my friend says. "They'll say they gave us a chance and we blew it."

One way to get some perspective on the QWL phenomenon is to recall the experiences of North American workers with company unions in the 1920s and early 1930s.

Then as now, the idea of greater participation by workers in the decisions that affect their lives was in the air. Then as now, corporate decisionmakers—the elderly white males who actually made the decisions and intended to go on doing so—devised schemes of seeming participation to coopt the impulse toward economic democracy. Then as now, the most insightful workers and their advocates in turn sought ways to use the workplace institutions sponsored by their bosses to their own advantage.

For example, George Patterson, a roll turner for U.S. Steel at its mill in South Chicago, recalled the following:

> The steel mill people came into the mill around 1933 and handed us a piece of paper. We looked at it, and it was called "An Employee Representation Plan." Now the Employee Representation Plan was the company union plan. It was based on the fact that we had the right to bargain collectively. The company drew the whole thing up, and the workers in various departments elected representatives of their own. I looked at this paper as a young lad and said, "This thing could never work," because it said right at the outset that there would be five members from management to sit on a committee and five members from the union—the company union—to sit on the committee. I asked who settled the tie, and of course I found out management did. So you see how useless it would have been.
>
> I talked to the fellows in the shop, and I talked faster than the others about unions. (I'd heard my dad talk about unions in the old country.) I said, "I don't think this thing is any good." So they elected me to be their representative! And the first thing I did was to begin to destroy this company union idea. I believed in the legitimate form of union. . . .
>
> So we formed an independent union. We tried to disband the company union, and we formed what we called the Associated Employees. This was just workers like myself attempting to do something by way of getting into a legitimate union.[1]

In the same way, workers today have a two-sided task in relation to QWL.

First they must unambiguously denounce the Mickey Mouse character of QWL as presently permitted by corporate boards of directors. In the words of the U.S. National Conference of Catholic Bishops: "Workers rightly reject calls for less adversarial relations when they are a smokescreen for demands that labor make all the concessions."[2]

Secondly, however, rather than simply turn their backs on QWL and practice wages-and-hours trade unionism in the traditional way, workers should make use of the rhetoric of QWL to demand a voice in the basic investment decisions that will determine the life or death of the places where they work.

This will require delicate tactical decisions and these will have to be made on a case-by-case basis: there is no one tactical formula for all situations in which QWL presents itself. Here we may fruitfully compare the similar movement for worker ownership. At one extreme there are ventures, such as Weirton Steel, where the common stock is owned by the workers but the board of directors—the majority of whom were chosen by the Wall Street investment firm Lazard Frères—runs the show and the workers, in order to keep the plant open, accepted a contract in which they promised not to strike for six years. (Yet even at Weirton, I am told, the workers appreciate the opportunity to make suggestions about their work that is provided by QWL groups.) At the other extreme is the situation like that at the Seymour Specialty Wire Company (in Seymour, Connecticut), where six of the nine members of the board of directors are elected by rank-and-file members of the union. Similarly, some worker-participation schemes will be more democratic than others. Different tactics will be called for in different situations.

Amidst tactical diversity, however, a simple strategic orientation must be kept clear: namely, that there will be no solution to the lack of democracy in North American corporations until private ownership is replaced by not-for-profit ownership, with maximum worker participation at all levels of decision-making, from shop floor to boardroom.

The great virtue of this book is that it recognizes what I have called the two-sided character of QWL. It shows how the QWL promise of workplace democracy is betrayed by the manipulation of QWL from above and its confinement to small-scale decisions about the immediate work setting. Above all, it shows how this contradiction can be overcome—transcended from within—by taking QWL rhetoric seriously and insisting on applying it to fundamental investment decisions.

Empty Promises makes three basic points. The first is that QWL has come about because of capitalism's need for increased profitability. For a firm like "Progress Motors," the pressure on profitability comes from the factors that Marx identified more than one hundred years ago. In order to remain competitive in an industry that has become increasingly global in production, massive new investment is required; this makes corporations squeeze their workers harder in order to maintain the same rate of profit as before.

Thus QWL does not mean that the capitalist leopard has changed its spots. Economic autocrats have not become democrats. Corporations continue to be more interested in meeting production goals than in the quality of the product. What is really going on is that the companies are desperate to increase the "productivity" of labor, or in words of one syllable, to make more dough from the same hours of work.

The second basic point made in *Empty Promises* is that QWL is not a process whereby management gives up power. On the contrary, QWL is intended to give management *more* power. "Management is no longer satisfied with making workers obey: it now wants them to *want* to obey." Management, through QWL, seeks "to tap the 'unemployed self,' the creative capacities of workers that managerial control has traditionally suppressed and wasted," but it does this not so that workers may express their human potentialities more fully, but so that management can dominate workers more completely. Thus QWL is the opposite of what it says it is.

In particular, as Wells shows, QWL is intended to undermine solidarity and to sow doubts among workers about the need for unions. Thus in 1981 General Motors circulated a confidential memo among its executives throughout North America encouraging them to use QWL programs to convince the workers that their union's collective bargaining demands were dangerous to the economic health of the company. As a result of QWL, workers are encouraged to blame, and punish, each other.

Third, according to *Empty Promises,* if workers want to fight QWL effectively they must do so by a vigorous drive "to make real the supposed ideals of QWL." Democracy in the workplace is labor's historical project, not management's. If management says it wants QWL and yet remains unbending and will not share power with the workers (and we know that this is how management *will* behave), then labor can put itself forward as the only force in a position to try to make QWL rhetoric into reality.

These basic ideas are illustrated by the two detailed case studies that the book presents.

Both at "Progress Motors" and at "Universal Electric," management turned to QWL when the plant was in trouble. At Progress Motors half the workforce had been on layoff for over a year before the introduction of QWL. At Universal Electric there was a general expectation that the plant was about to close, and this is in fact what happened—QWL notwithstanding. The results of QWL were largely negative at both plants. The speed of the line at Progress Motors was increased by a third. At both plants, management refused to go along with suggestions that would have cost significant amounts of money. (Therefore, for example, the suggestion for an enclosed eating area in the Paint Shop was turned down.) To the extent that QWL had partial successes, these were often at the expense of workers in other departments and thus weakened union solidarity. The union was weakened in another way at Progress Motors because the "quality boosters," who were chosen by management to oversee the quality of work, were often former union militants.

This brings us to the final message of Donald Wells' challenging book: if labor is successfully to cope with QWL, it is the unions themselves that will have to change. QWL is attractive to workers because it holds out the promise that they will be treated with dignity, that their ideas will be valued, that they can be part of a group of equals working toward a common goal. This experience is presently denied to workers both by companies and by unions. North American trade unions are typically centralized, bureaucratic structures, staffed by full-time representatives who have long since forgotten what it was like to work on the shop floor. Unions frequently make decisions *for* workers, not *with* them; still less do critical decisions about unions get made *by* workers. It is true that union locals are often relatively democratic, but locals do not make national union policy. It is true that most national unions submit contracts for rank-and-file ratification and elect national officers by referendum. But unions cultivate a siege mentality, in which any party in opposition to the incumbent administration is perceived as traitorous; in this atmosphere, democratic mechanisms cannot function freely.

The North American union has become especially weak on the shop floor, which, in the words of *Empty Promises,* is the unions' Achilles heel. Where there should be a steward for every foreman, elected at frequent intervals, recallable at will, and obliged to rotate out of office after one (or a few) terms; where rank-and-file workers should retain the power to settle problems on the shop floor by group pressure and action; where the union's grassroots level should be the informal work group—where all this should be, there is instead all too often a vacuum at the shop-floor level, a vacuum that can be seductively filled by the warm, people-respecting rhetoric of QWL and the shop-floor groups and committees through which it functions. As Don Wells comments, developing ways to cement the ties between local union leaders and rank-and-file members is in the long run the most crucial task of all.

Labor's supporters and advocates outside the plant also have an important role to play in overcoming and transcending QWL. *Empty Promises* accurately notes that it is frequently the left of the political mainstream in Canada and the United States that has called for softer approaches to management, in the name of national "competitiveness" and social unity. Intellectuals allied to the labor movement should at least perform the minimal function of contributing to intellectual clarity. In the case of QWL, this means exposing the empty promises of QWL and instead projecting the first sketches of what a genuine economic democracy might look like.

The labor movement is fighting for its life, and its future will depend in part on its response to QWL.

Notes

1. George Patterson, "Your Dog Don't Bark No More," in Alice and Staughton Lynd, eds., *Rank and File: Personal Histories by Working-Class Organizers* (Princeton, N.J.: Princeton University Press, 1981), pp. 91–92.
2. *Economic Justice for All: Pastoral Letter on Catholic Social Teaching and the U.S. Economy* (1986), p. 150.

Preface

This book results from an unusually cooperative collective effort. I am grateful to over two hundred workers at "Progress Motors" and "Universal Electric" for helping me to understand their experiences during the implementation of a number of Quality of Working Life (QWL) programs. Many of them also helped me to design questionnaires, which they and others then answered. Thanks also go to many members of management in both plants. I am grateful, as well, for the advice and insights of over a hundred leaders from the following unions: Aluminum, Brick and Glass Workers' Union; Amalgamated Clothing and Textile Workers' Union; Brotherhood of Railway Carmen; Canadian Airline Employees' Association; Canadian Automobile Workers; Canadian Paperworkers' Union; Canadian Union of Postal Workers; Canadian Union of Public Employees; Canadian Union of United Brewery and Distillery Workers; Communications and Electrical Workers of Canada; Energy and Chemical Workers' Union; International Association of Machinists; International Brotherhood of Electrical Workers; International Ladies Garment Workers' Union; Ontario Public Service Employees' Union; Public Service Alliance of Canada; Retail, Wholesale and Department Store Union; United Food and Commercial Workers; and United Steelworkers of America.

For their advice and assistance, I am especially indebted to Jane Armstrong, Ed Birkland, Gary Bromby, Pat Clancy, Ian Curtin, Gary Forget, Sam Gindin, Stephen Herzenberg, Gerry Hunnius, Barry Johnston, Terry Leeson, D'Arcy Martin, Bruce May, Mac McNair, Al Paquette, Kevin Park, Mike Parker, Jim Rinehart, and Jim Turk. I am also especially indebted to the late

Jack de Boer, whose work in this area awakened my own interest in these issues and served as a guide for my own research. Special thanks are due to Joe Grogan for his unstinting support throughout the entire project. Thanks go as well to the Centre for Labour Studies Advisory Committee of the Labour Council of Metropolitan Toronto, and in particular to Wally Majesky and Mike Lyons. I am also grateful to Barbara Vilneff for typing earlier drafts of this book. Above all, this book has benefited from innumerable contributions made by Ruth Frager. She was centrally involved in every aspect of research and writing.

Research for this book was funded by a grant from Labour Canada to the Centre for Labour Studies, Humber College. Tom McAulay, technical advisor in Quality of Working Life, Labour Canada, helped to administer the grant and gave useful advice regarding the project.

The information in this book would have been far less accessible had it not been for the painstaking and tactful efforts of David Cubberley, of the Brotherhood of Railway and Airline Clerks, to make my prose clearer and more interesting. I am also grateful to Susan Lowes, of Monthly Review Press, who edited this book. It is entirely due to her suggestions that I completely reorganized the original manuscript and added new material, making the book much more comprehensive and coherent.

—Donald Wells

Toronto, May 1987

EMPTY PROMISES

1

An Introduction to QWL

Trade unionism in the United States and Canada stands at a crossroads. In one direction lie contemporary versions of any old dream: the revitalization of organized labor as a social movement struggling alongside other progressive social forces to create a more democratic workplace and a more democratic society. In the other direction lies a new alliance between labor and capital, based on a new industrial relations system which features workers and managers in a close cooperative relationship in the workplace. Proponents of this second direction maintain that it too will result in greater democracy: *management* will give workers a much greater say on the job, which will mean not only a democratic workplace, but also a more genuinely democratic society—in short, a more benign kind of capitalism. It will also mean a more productive capitalism: according to this scenario, such cooperation between labor and management holds the key to the kind of increased productivity that can make the United States and Canada competitive, once again, in the international marketplace. This scenario thus combines a vision of genuine equality with a tough-minded dollars-and-cents practicality. The rising sun on this anticipated bright new day for both capitalists and workers is the programs called "Quality of Working Life," or QWL.

A great many different workplace innovations come under the QWL banner. Many QWL programs are associated with various kinds of job redesign, such as "job rotation" (workers perform different jobs in sequence), "job enlargement" or "horizontal loading" (two or more jobs of similar nature are combined), "job enrichment" or "vertical loading" (the upgrading of jobs to include greater skill and responsibility), and "autonomous work groups" (where groups of workers have greater collective responsibility for the organization of their work). To one degree or another, such restructuring implies a reversal (although not a wholesale rejection) of the basic direction of the organization of work in this century: the removal of much of workers' ability to plan their work, and the replacement of more complex and skilled jobs with job fragments that allow management detailed control over workers.

In addition to the common association between QWL and this kind of job redesign, QWL programs are always characterized by their focus on greater participation by workers, usually through labor-management committees. The structures and decision-making processes of these committees vary considerably. So do the names for QWL programs: among others, these include "employee involvement programs," "quality circles," "participative management," "joint labor-management councils," "participative problem solving," "team management," and "labor-management participation."

No matter what name they go by, however, all QWL programs embody an orientation to conflict in the workplace that is fundamentally psychological: most of the existing barriers to cooperation between management and labor are believed to derive from the distorted images the two sides have of each other, and the fears associated with these images. Power relations in the workplace are seen as *personal* conflicts—"adolescent," or even socially deviant. QWL exponents believe that if these psychological barriers can be understood and overcome, workers and managers will see that they have more in common than either ever knew, and that they will discover a whole new way of cooperating for their mutual benefit. This therapeutic framework is the essential QWL rationale.

While management is supposed to benefit from major productivity increases, QWL consultants argue that there is an equivalent payoff for workers in the form of better jobs, greater job satisfaction, and greater job security. These mutual benefits are held to be a matter of common sense: since it is workers who do the jobs, it is workers who know more than anyone else about how to make those jobs more productive. If, therefore, managers give workers more say about their jobs, and if workers understand that they have a personal stake in making their jobs more productive, everyone will gain. Workers who have more say on the job—and better jobs as a result—are bound to be happier workers. It is an axiom in personnel relations that happier workers are more productive workers: they work harder, they are more loyal to management, they need less supervision, and they have lower rates of absenteeism, sickness, and on-the-job accidents. Not least in importance, greater productivity often implies greater profits and hence more investment to create more jobs. Exponents of QWL see this as the basic logic of a "win-win" relationship between labor and capital. QWL is thus the matchmaker in a new marriage between two old enemies, profit and democracy.

In daily practice, QWL programs focus on the myriad of on-the-job problems that normally bedevil any attempt at such matchmaking. It is the task of QWL groups (or circles or teams) to work out these problems at their weekly or biweekly meetings. The teams are normally made up of between three and twelve workers, along with their supervisors and other management personnel. They often include a trained QWL coordinator, frequently someone who is well versed in the social psychology of small groups. In some QWL programs, participation is up to the individual worker; in others, workers may decide by majority vote that everyone in the department or zone is to take part. In still other cases, participation is restricted to a few worker representatives and designated management personnel. The way the meetings are run also varies: whereas some are taken up almost entirely with solving specific problems, others consist of far less structured discussions about a wide range of workplace issues. No matter how the QWL teams are chosen and no matter how they operate, they are designed to undermine the sense of conflict between "them" and "us" that exists between workers and bosses.

The cooperation between workers and managers in these

meetings is supposed to foster a more general cooperation outside the meetings: the whole point of QWL is to create a new kind of cooperation on the job. Traditional bossing is to give way to a situation in which workers supervise themselves and each other. Workers' knowledge about their jobs is to be put at the disposal of the QWL groups and applied to productivity improvements. Oppressive jobs are to be redesigned by the QWL teams so that they are more varied, the workers' mental and physical abilities are better used, and the jobs become meaningful and enjoyable. This is the QWL promise.

Although QWL programs are spreading to all kinds of workplaces—an estimated one in seven of all American firms with over one hundred workers and two in five with over five hundred workers—they are most often found in the largest corporations, especially those on the leading edge of the economy where management techniques are most sophisticated.* An inside estimate is that between one-third and one-half of the "Fortune 500" firms are now involved in some version of QWL, a massive increase in only a few years. QWL programs are especially popular in industries whose profit margins are being narrowed by heightened international competition (as in the

*Among some of the better known organizations with QWL programs are Alcan, Alcoa, American Telephone & Telegraph, Atlantic Richfield, Bankers Trust, Baxter Travenol Laboratories, Bell Telephone, Bethlehem Steel, Borg-Warner, Citibank, Corning, Dana, Digital, Eastern Airlines, Eaton, Ebasco Services, Exxon, Fireman's Fund Insurance, Ford, General Electric, General Foods, General Motors, Harley-Davidson, Heinz, Hewlett Packard, Honeywell, Hughes Aircraft, Inland Steel, International Business Machines, Kaiser Aluminum and Chemical, Kroger's, Lear Siegler, Lockheed, Manufacturers Hanover Trust, Metropolitan Life, Minnesota Mining and Manufacturing, Monsanto, Nabisco, Northrop Corporation, Pillsbury, Polaroid, P.P.G. Industries, Procter and Gamble, Prudential Insurance, Ralston Purina, San Francisco General Hospital, Security Pacific National Bank, Shaklee Corporation, State of Ohio Department of Highways, Sun Chemical, Texas Instruments, Westinghouse, Weyerhauser, and Xerox.

manufacturing sector) and in industries where complex and costly technological changes are being introduced. QWL programs are also common in workplaces such as chemical plants and oil refineries, where modern continuous-flow process technology makes production vulnerable to expensive breakdowns. Finally, QWL programs are concentrated in those parts of the service sector where the new microchip technology is being introduced (such as airlines, supermarkets, postal services, telephone companies, banks, and insurance companies), and where the quality of service is often hard to quantify, hard to monitor, and highly dependent on worker morale (such as hospitals, schools, hotels, prisons, and the military).

Employers such as these, many of whom are facing profit and budget constraints, often present QWL to their workers as a kind of substitute for better pay and benefits. This tradeoff between economic concessions and "political" concessions implies a reversal of the pattern of collective bargaining: until recently, most employers have been willing to agree to wage and benefit increases as long as "management's rights" to make the important decisions about the organization of work were kept off the bargaining table. Now that there is less money to quell worker discontent, that taboo is being lifted—or so workers and union leaders are being told.

It is precisely the relationship between QWL programs and management rights that is the key issue. Are managers really giving up some of their power? Does this new type of industrial relations provide an opening for genuine cooperation between workers and management, based on greater equality between the two? As the two case studies that form the basis of this book show, the answer is no. Not only does QWL *not* provide such an opening, but it actually *increases* management power. The result is less equality between labor and management, less democracy in the workplace. As a consequence, QWL (ironically) *reduces* the quality of working life. In the end, QWL is simply a softer, subtler management-control strategy, yet one that is more ambitious and all-embracing than anything seen before. Management is no longer satisfied with making workers obey: it now wants them to *want* to obey. This is the real significance of QWL.

It is no mere coincidence that QWL consultants use essentially the same techniques that are taught to executives in "union-free management" seminars. Nor is it a coincidence that QWL programs are part of a resurgence of "soft" supervisory techniques, where smiles, slaps on the back, questions about how the kids are doing, and other kinds of manipulation replace shouts and threats as a means of getting the work done. QWL is often introduced along with individual and group monetary incentive schemes, including profit-sharing plans and "productivity-sharing" plans, which tend to reinforce individualism and undermine worker solidarity. Similarly, QWL programs are frequently implemented along with "employee assistance programs," which are aimed at helping workers deal with their (productivity-reducing) problems of anxiety, alcohol use, depression, drug dependency, and so on. Workers are persuaded that these problems are "personal" problems not related to the workplace, but problems that management nevertheless cares enough about to lend a hand. (The most conservative figures indicate that comprehensive employee assistance programs return $2.00 or $3.00 in increased productivity for every $1.00 spent. A recent conference on employee assistance programs included a session titled "Who's the Client?")

Wrapping themselves in a shroud of vague language about the need for "openness and trust," for "self-actualization," and "for new adaptiveness," the proponents of QWL are quick to say that *their* program is not the manipulative thing its critics call it, but slow indeed to tell us in any concrete way what it actually is. Although these highly paid experts have fine-tuned the procedures for introducing QWL into the workplace, their sales pitch and the vast literature promoting QWL are curiously imprecise. All too often the initial acceptance of QWL by the workers requires what amounts to blind faith in its promises, in the QWL consultants, and above all in management. Because of this, the fervent missionary zeal of QWL advocates becomes in practice a pretentious, expensive, and complicated con job.

The high-sounding claims made about QWL provide a major clue to its problems. Not only do QWL advocates promise the kinds of jobs that only fools would turn down—jobs offering "enjoyment," "accomplishment," "pride," "optimal variety," "challenge and ongoing opportunities to learn," and "real decision-making responsibilities and power"—but on top of all this they are offering what workers have always been refused: the rule of "democratic principles in the workplace" based on "joint control and shared responsibility between union and management at all levels."

It is through this kind of "cooperation" that businesses and governments are trying to find a substitute for the adversarial relationship that gives rise to genuine trade unionism. The irreparable flaw in this attempt at engineered cooperation is that while business and government have a great deal to gain, workers have much to lose—including the leverage in the workplace that makes trade unionism possible.

This new type of industrial relations is an attempt to make a virtue out of new necessities. The United States has lost its once absolute dominance, not only over competitors in Western Europe and Japan but even in relation to some of the third world power centers, especially those on the Pacific Rim. This redivision of the world economy has occurred in the context of an accelerating shift of capital investment by an increasing number of globally integrated corporations and banks. It has been accompanied by massive corporate restructuring, in the form of merger and joint-production agreements, as well as by various kinds of corporate divorce, divestment, and other sorts of organizational disintegration. On top of this, a new wave of technological change is hastening economic dislocation. With unparalleled swiftness, entire (generally labor-intensive) industries are dying and new (often capital-intensive) ones are being born, as

Canada and the United States enter the era of deindustrialization. This, combined with a powerful squeeze on profits and massive unemployment, has devastated the industrial heartlands and shifted the centers of economic and political power from the Northeastern "rust-belts" of the organized U.S. working class to the anti-union and low-wage Southern "sun-belt" and the West. As a result, we are witnessing an historic shift in the balance of forces between workers and employers.

In the midst of this topsy-turvy political economy, innovations in industrial relations have become a critical factor in the fight for economic survival. Since the rate of growth of the economy is no longer sufficient to provide the ever larger national income "pie" that has until now been big enough to buy off class conflict, employers have mobilized for a massive offensive against workers. In the late 1970s and early 1980s that offensive was directed against the labor movement in the guise of a war on inflation. At the same time, the employers' offensive continues to have another front and another rationale. More than ever before, management longs not only to reduce workers' wages and benefits but also to tap the "unemployed self," the creative capacities of workers that managerial control has traditionally suppressed and wasted. It is QWL that promises access to this potential source of productivity.

For example, where costly technology is the price that has to be paid to meet international competition, and where it needs to be introduced very rapidly, the *active* cooperation of workers in the transition can make the margin of difference between survival and bankruptcy. Where the new technology requires a smaller, more flexible workforce to meet optimum production levels, QWL programs also give employers a way to get workers to commit themselves to the redesign of the work, even though that may well lead to their being laid off. Thus, QWL is used to get workers to pursue productivity goals and at the same time pay the costs of a management offensive against them—an offensive that workers might otherwise resist. QWL is, in effect, an attempt at redefining what it means to manage—and what it means to submit.

This new type of industrial relations is about more than management's response to a specific economic crisis, however. It is also about the ways political and economic elites are responding to domestic social disintegration. The end of Pax Americana and the longest period of sustained economic growth and almost full employment in modern history threatens the competitive individualism, the acquisitiveness and consumerism that have for so long provided Americans with a sense of collective identity and purpose. Today we are witnessing a resurgence of national chauvinism and appeals to social solidarity against *external* enemies: Russia (the Evil Empire), Libya and Iran (the terrorist nations), Japan and the European Economic Community (the unfair competitors), and much of the third world (the ungrateful debtors). The appeals, especially in the United States, are to a new national harmony, the elimination of *internal* conflicts—and nowhere is that more important to political and economic elites than in the workplace, the cradle of productivity and profits—and worker resistance.

Because it promises to make the workplace more cooperative, QWL promises not only renewed economic competitiveness but also a more democratic society. QWL extends the image of democracy from the ballot box into the workplace, and that image of an economic complement to political democracy resonates with strong populist currents in the political cultures of both Canada and the United States.

As this study shows, however, QWL in fact means moving further away from economic democracy and toward greater management control. The history of modern management is a history of increasing management control through masking management power, and QWL is the latest disguise. Instead of embedding control in the technology of production (as Henry Ford did with his assembly line), or in impersonal bureaucratic rules concerning job evaluations, "merit" increases, promotion and pay ladders, and all the rest of it (as in the modern union contract), QWL attempts to hide the supervisor in the worker's head. To the extent that management is able to implant its own ideology among workers, QWL represents the furthest point management has reached along the frontier of control in the workplace—the battle for workers' minds.

This study is an attempt to understand this battle by examining the worker's own experience of QWL. It provides an objective, factual account of how well QWL measures up to its promise of better, more secure jobs, and of a greater say for workers. It also provides an evaluation of the impact QWL has on worker solidarity, on the ability to fight back, and on the quality of the unions.

The core of this evaluation lies in case studies of what QWL has meant for workers in two quite different settings. These examples were selected specifically because they represent QWL at its best: they therefore allow analysis of these programs in their own best light.

The first of these programs was started in 1980 in a sprawling, technologically up-to-date automobile assembly plant in Canada owned by Progress Motors (a fictitious name for one of the Big Three U.S. automakers). This program was soon deemed so successful that it became the showpiece of the Ontario government's Quality of Working Life Centre, an internationally renowned agency whose purpose is to install QWL programs in unionized workplaces. The second program was set up in 1981 at a large, multiproduct electronics plant owned by Universal Electric (a pseudonym for a major U.S.-owned multinational). It was devised and started by one of the foremost private QWL consultants, and it too represents one of the most sophisticated programs currently available. Yet despite prodigious advantages, neither program can be regarded as a success.

These programs were chosen for analysis not only because they represent QWL at its best but also because they represent distinctly different versions of it. Whereas the "quality circles" at Universal Electric operated according to specific and quite rigid "problem-solving" procedures, the QWL groups at Progress Motors made up their own agenda and style of decision-making as they went along. The groups themselves were also different: at Universal they were made up of volunteers, while at Progress they were composed of workers elected to represent their work areas. Whereas senior and middle management at Universal were an integral part of the groups, at Progress only front-line supervision took part.

These contrasting programs also show how QWL varies between different kinds of workplaces. At Universal there was an enormous diversity in the labor process: much of the work was done at individual machines or at separate workbenches using a wide variety of tools and techniques. The range of products and technologies used was also extensive. At Progress, by contrast, automobiles were the sole product, and almost all of the employees performed uniformly regulated jobs on an assembly line. Partly as a result of this uniformity in production, industrial relations at Progress were also more homogeneous, and there was only one union. At Universal, on the other hand, there were five unions and consequently a much greater variation in pay and benefits, promotions, discipline, and working conditions. There was also greater variation in the unions' attitudes toward QWL.

These examples were chosen from among more than twenty programs that were considered "mature" (where QWL had been in effect for several years) and where both management and the union agreed to cooperate. Much of what follows is based on interviews. Their sequence reflected the requirements of bureaucratic protocol: I began at the top of each hierarchy by conducting extensive interviews with union leaders and senior company management at the national level. I then interviewed plant-level management, the consultants who had helped to implement the programs, and the local union leadership. Next I interviewed those union stewards and front-line supervisors who were involved in various ways with the programs. After all these interviews had been completed, I began to interview the workers who were participating in the programs.

All the interviews were informal and open-ended, their content and length varying according to the individual's role in the programs. I introduced myself as an academic doing a study of QWL, and made it clear that I had no definite preconceptions about these programs but that I was simply interested in understanding the "facts." Each interview was conducted on a one-on-one basis, with as much privacy as possible, and I promised that information given me would be confidential in the sense that neither the individual's nor the company's name would be published. Partly to allay any further concerns about confidentiality, I did not use a tape recorder but made notes, both during each interview and afterward.

Using information from these interviews, together with agreements and memoranda between union and management, QWL training manuals, grievance data, supervisors' logbooks, and my own observations of QWL meetings, I constructed chronologies of events, organizational frameworks, and QWL decision-making processes in order to get an overview. Next I constructed questionnaires that would assess the impact of the programs on job satisfaction, supervisory practices, the workers' feelings of identification with the companies and the quality of the products they were making, efficiency of production, job descriptions, working conditions, relations with union leaders and fellow workers, the resolution of labor-management conflicts, the workers' feelings about job security, and much else. These lengthy questionnaires were distributed to every worker who participated in the program, and to about the same number of those who did not. They were normally filled out on the spot, during a work break. At Universal, the results were supplemented by an attitudinal survey that management had previously conducted.

I also conducted follow-up interviews with some of the workers, generally at their homes. I did further interviews with managers and local union leaders, as well as with white-collar workers at Universal who were participating in the quality circles. Finally, I distributed a draft of the evaluation and invited criticisms. Although several suggestions for the correction of details were offered, everyone I asked—managers, union leaders, workers—agreed with the overall findings.

Since both case studies showed that the programs had failed, this consensus was the most surprising result of all.

The reason seems to be that the QWL programs do not fulfill the promises they make to either management *or* workers. Thus both are disappointed, but for different reasons. Further, the problems that were revealed are not amenable to being fixed by tinkering: it is not a matter of devising a *better* QWL program. The problems go deeper than that, and are ultimately insoluble: they lie in the premise that labor and management can find a genuine basis of cooperation while their basic relationship—the domination of workers by bosses—remains the same.

The critical point is this: QWL is the opposite of what it says it is. Virtually every improvement in job conditions has come from the workers' ability to band together to protect themselves. This is why unions arose in the first place. The adversarial relationship between labor and management does not derive from some historical accident or from a colossal misunderstanding that "better communications" or a "more mature approach" can resolve. It stems from the fact that businesses survive by beating their competitors—and, other things being equal, this means squeezing as much as possible out of workers. Unions did not cause this conflict; they arose as a response to it. QWL, too, is a response to this conflict—but it is management's response.

As this study shows in detail, QWL is part of management's response to new technologies and changing economic conditions, and is essentially designed to achieve greater power for management: power over the workers, over the way they work, and over the product of their labor. It is meant to undermine solidarity and to sow doubts about the need for unions. It is the heart of a new industrial relations system that threatens to do away with the gains labor has made since the 1930s.

Beyond providing a critique of QWL in its own terms, this book sets out a strategy for developing genuine improvement in the quality of working life. It starts from the proposition that at least one thing is certain: too many powerful people have too much to gain for this new type of industrial relations to disappear just because workers are wary of it or because union leaders would like to ignore it. The only strategy available to most organized workers is to use the collective bargaining process, and their own solidarity, to initiate a vigorous drive—a workers' drive—to make real the supposed ideals of QWL.

This strategy recognizes a great irony: workers want better and more secure jobs, they want dignity and more democracy in the workplace—and they always have. After all, this is labor's history, a history in which business and government have typically opposed these goals. Now business and government want "QWL." This irony can be an important opening for labor. If management *says* it wants QWL and yet *in fact* remains unbending and will not share power with the workers, then management's support for the promises of QWL will prove false. If, on the other hand, trade unionists can use their collective strength to gain genuine improvements in the quality of their working lives, then a better era of industrial relations could be at hand. For this to happen, workers need to know the difference between high-sounding ideals and plain facts, between QWL as a public relations gimmick and real improvements in the quality of working life. At this point, QWL is a potentially devastating management weapon, but its promises of a more humane workplace can be turned to labor's favor. We need to understand QWL as both a great peril and a great opportunity if we are to move toward a genuinely cooperative workplace, a more productive economy, and a fundamentally democratic society.

2

The Rise and Fall of QWL at Progress Motors

Assembling automobiles is one of the most boring jobs any human being can do. Consider, for example, the job of disc grinding. The worker huddles inside a sheet-metal box about twenty feet long by perhaps twelve feet wide. The assembly line lumbers steadily, inexorably, through the box, carrying an endless procession of brown and gray metal skeletons. Each time a skeleton comes by, the worker picks up a portable grinder—his or her only tool—and presses it onto three or four bubbled welds, grinding them smooth in a screech of metal against metal. That is it. A step forward, then a shuffle backward for a couple of feet as the line pushes him along, then a couple of steps to the left and a shuffle with the line back to where it starts all over again. At Progress Motors, the disc grinder does this "job" forty-eight times an hour, ten hours a day. Incessantly.

That is what assembly-line work is like for most of the workers at the Progress Motors plant, a corrugated city of long, low, boxlike buildings strung out over sixty acres of flat fields next to an expressway. Cameras scan the parking lots. Inside, the main buildings are like enormous half-lit caves of metal and cement covering a maze of aisles of assembly lines, machines, and stacks of spare parts. The main line zigs and zags through the plant like a gigantic intestine, surrounded by a host of smaller subassembly lines, and by overhead conveyors on which doors and other parts hang like carcasses.

There is mass anonymity. The more than six thousand work-

15

ers in this particular plant become numbers. In fact, each has two: a punch-clock number to be paid by, and a seniority number to be laid off by. There is widespread job insecurity because this plant is part of an industry in crisis. It is predicted that up to half the auto industry's North American workforce will be laid off by the end of the decade and that more will be lost by the year 2000. This loss of jobs will be the result of a sharp increase in foreign competition and the global integration of the industry combined with the saturation of much of the industry's consumer market and the arrival of new labor-saving technologies. At this plant, more than half the workforce was recently on layoff for over a year. Although most of the workers have now been called back, there remains a profound anxiety about job security, even among those with ten or fifteen years' seniority.

It is important to bear all this in mind as we try to understand why the workers and union leaders became involved in QWL, for these are precisely the conditions that QWL is supposed to change: it promises to provide good jobs, secure jobs. It is supposed to mean that workers become "somebodies," that they take part in democratic decision-making in the plant.

Years before, as a response to the "new breed of worker" whose increasing militancy emerged in the late 1960s and early 1970s—symbolized most notably by the strike at the General Motors plant in Lordstown, Ohio, in 1972—employers in the automobile industry had begun to experiment with various worker participation programs which they hoped would overcome these conditions. The early model for such programs was based on schemes already underway in Sweden. In addition to providing some environmental improvements, these schemes attempted to improve the workers' attitudes toward their supervisors. In Sweden, their most ambitious aspect was the replacement of the traditional assembly line with "semi-autonomous" groups of workers who were given considerable collective discretion about how they did their work.

With notions like these in mind as a solution to their employees' "blue collar blues"—to their long, bitter strikes, their much publicized walkouts, their increasing tendency to quit their jobs, their mounting absenteeism, their accelerating grievance rates, and their increasing resort to sabotage—North American automakers began QWL discussions with national leaders of the United Auto Workers (UAW) during the 1973 contract negotiations. While the UAW agreed to become involved in QWL efforts, and while both General Motors and Ford set up QWL programs in several plants, many of these programs quickly failed. It was not until demand improved in the late 1970s that QWL was once again given a higher position on the corporate agenda. And it was not until the massive increase in foreign competition in the early 1980s, combined with increasing consumer awareness of the poor quality of North American cars, that management showed a strong interest in QWL as a way to cut production costs and improve not only worker morale but also their corporate image.

Thus, all along, QWL was a response to management's varying needs. Although a formal agreement to install QWL had been in place since the early 1970s, the actual implementation of QWL at this Progress Motors plant did not take place until the early 1980s. Indeed, it was not until thousands of workers in the plant were on indefinite layoff that QWL took its first small and tentative steps onto the plant floor, a child of industrial crisis.

Steering QWL from the Top Down

The national UAW leadership opened the way for QWL, but it was the local leadership that was left to work out the details with management. This was done with the help of consultants from the provincial government's Quality of Working Life Centre. According to the center's mandate, both management and union must agree to begin such projects before the center can become involved. Though the consultants at the center are clearly partisans of QWL, they do not present themselves as allies of either management or labor, but rather as knowledgeable mediators. In addition to expertise, the center provides funding to cover some of the costs of starting the program. As a source of cash, expertise, and reassurance, the center's consultants therefore have great authority, especially at the beginning of a project.

As a first step, top plant management and senior leaders from the union met separately with the QWL consultants to discuss how to proceed. Several months later the consultants proposed a decision-making structure that was acceptable to both sides. Its chief element was a joint board, dubbed the "steering committee," composed of four key leaders of the union and four key members of management. The significant feature of this steering committee was that it formally empowered *both* sides to oversee the development of the QWL project. This meant that each side had the right to veto proposals made by the other, *and* that each side had the right to veto any initiative coming from the plant floor.

The steering committee's supremacy was joined to two other conditions that the union insisted on. First, no jobs were to be lost as a result of the QWL project. Second, the project was not to interfere with the provisions of the collective bargaining agreement. Plant managers agreed orally to both conditions but refused to give a written, legally binding guarantee that jobs would not be lost. The union leaders accepted these promises, some because they felt that they were given in good faith, others because they felt that the real force that would hold management to the agreement was the union's option of withdrawing from the project at any time. "How could we lose?" one union leader asked.

Thus the first phase brought senior decision-makers from the union and management together to create a structure within which QWL could develop. Final authority remained at the top, in the labor-management steering committee. Therefore, even though the QWL program had been initiated through collective bargaining, it was to be implemented by a new structure that lay outside the collective bargaining framework, one that was not even under the direct influence of the rest of the local leadership or membership, most of whom had only a vague notion of what it was all about. Their support, where it existed at all, was passive. In sum, then, it was at the prompting of government officials, national union officers, and senior corporate executives that selected leaders of the local union helped to initiate a decision-making framework, the core of which was a promise to broaden the rank-and-file workers' control over their jobs.

An Experimental Beginning

The steering committee was nothing if not cautious in bringing QWL to the plant floor. After considerable deliberation, it chose the Trim Zone, an area with about twenty workers and one supervisor, as the site for a pilot project. The chief attraction of Trim was that it was a "good" zone where the workers and their supervisor got along exceptionally well. The choice was also consistent with the advice of the QWL consultants, who "guidelined the union reps to the conclusion of not going to the bad zones," a union member of the steering committee reported. He recalled that the supervisor in Trim was considered particularly well suited for the experiment since he was widely known to be "fair to deal with, provided he had the autonomy to do it." In addition, the union steward in Trim served on the steering committee and was a visible supporter of QWL.

While unusual in these respects, Trim was nonetheless very much like other zones in the most fundamental sense—the design of the work. Workers in Trim install such items as door handles and windshield wipers and are paced by the steady, relentless movement of the line. Like most workers in the plant (all but a handful of whom are men), each worker in this zone repeats his task an average of once every 1.3 minutes. If QWL could do anything to improve these jobs, its appeal to the workers would clearly be enormous.

Once the steering committee had chosen Trim, all twenty men who worked there were approached. They were asked to spend Friday evening and Saturday at a QWL orientation session at a nearby "luxury" hotel. Their expenses would be taken care of, they would be paid as if they were working at the plant, and the environment would be more than pleasant—a jovial, fraternity-house sort of boys' night out with the bosses. Not surprisingly, everyone agreed.

At the orientation session, the consultants described the attractions of the project in vague terms: greater variety in the work and more desirable jobs, more "elbow room," a chance to learn, and an opportunity to improve relations with others. This was an appealing outline that each worker could fill in for himself. "For years we didn't listen to the workers," one worker remembered a manager saying. "Now we think a better worker is more cooperative. If we listen to workers, we'll get a better quality product." The emphasis of the union members on the steering committee was somewhat different. They explained that the real purpose of the program was to improve the quality of working life, just as the name implied, and that any changes in product quality would be a "spin-off," not the main goal. The description of QWL was so alluring that some workers came away with the impression that it had been "forced" on management during the latest contract negotiations.

As a result of this session, the pilot project was welcomed by the workers in Trim, although the welcome was tinged with skepticism, the result of memories of heavy-handed management actions in the past. Despite this, it appeared to the workers that there was little to be lost and much to be gained: better jobs, perhaps; more dignity; maybe even a chance to avoid further layoffs.

The workers in Trim unanimously agreed to elect three of their own as representatives to what was called the "project committee," a structure that had been proposed by the consultants and accepted by the steering committee. No attempt was made to make these representatives formally accountable to their constituents: the worker representatives were not elected on the basis of any specific platform, no limits were set on their terms of office, and there was no formal mechanism for their recall. The committee's purpose was to take suggestions from the shop floor, decide on their merits and priority, and bring them to the steering committee in the form of workable proposals. The steering committee would have the final say.

The project committee was thus, from the outset, wholly subordinate to the steering committee, and its recommendations could be overridden. It was clearly designed to be controlled from above, but the workers who were elected to it, and those who elected them, had not been made aware of this at the orientation meeting.

The project committee also included the steward and the zone supervisor, who provided a second set of links to senior management and to the union leadership. After the orientation weekend, five members of the project committee (the three elected workers, plus the steward and the supervisor) attended further workshops held by the consultants. The chairperson of the project committee (one of the worker representatives) also attended workshops with members of the steering committee and other union members and managers.

Such were the ties that bound the project committee to the hierarchies above it. From the start there was little chance that the project would develop in any direction that management could not control. As we shall see, however, the union did not enjoy the same prerogative.

Back in Trim, members of the project committee enthusiastically canvassed the workers for suggestions of ways to improve their working life. There were numerous proposals, including voluntary job rotation, the elimination of punch clocks, more sweepers, a more equitable distribution of workloads, and the introduction of piped-in music. Further suggestions were gathered at another workshop outside the plant, this one organized by the QWL Centre. Here workers were taught a few problem-solving techniques; they in turn asked to learn more about how the company made production decisions. The result was that management arranged for yet another meeting with the workers at which several managers described how their roles fit into the decision-making process in the plant as a whole. Much of what was said may not have been clearly understood, but the workers came away believing that their participation in QWL fit into a larger picture, that their work was part of a major cooperative effort. This belief gave many of them a greater sense of identification with management.

Most of the workers in Trim thus responded favorably to this early phase of the project. They took the orientation sessions seriously, and they appreciated the extra pay and the time to get to know their managers and each other in comfortable and relaxed circumstances. It was during this period that the workers developed a much firmer sense of group identity. Many also appreciated the respectful way in which management was soliciting their opinions. Some felt a greater self-confidence as a result of the new sense of equality they had with some of their bosses.

This was especially true of the workers' relationship to their immediate supervisor. Unlike the more typical supervisor who acted like a sergeant-major in boot camp, issuing threats and heaping abuse on recalcitrant workers, the supervisor in Trim was courteous, considerate, and helpful. His policy was to settle problems before they became major issues, thereby avoiding having to force the workers to resort to the grievance procedure. Consequently, he was liked and respected throughout the zone—this was one of the main reasons Trim had been chosen for the pilot project in the first place.

Prior to the QWL project, most of the workers had cooperated with this supervisor by working to an acceptable standard, a more or less passive compliance. After the project was set up, their cooperation with the supervisor increased dramatically because many of the workers *actively* sought ways to improve production in the zone. The supervisor was amazed. "My job is so much easier that it's disgusting," he said, showing me a logbook he had made at the time. The following entries appeared over several months:

Fred giving more of himself to help himself. Morton aggressively helpful. Fred called me twice now about breakdowns before they became major. Peter has kept word and not missing a shift, thank goodness. Vendor defects getting good attention.

Breakdown this A.M. but Antonio reported the [indication of breakdown] and we covered without mishap. He stated, "I never would have reported that in the old days." Just one small incident.

Dimitri called me to [a location]—[a unit] was side-tipped on the line with a garbage box. Anyhow, Sigmund went off platform, moved the box, and saved system damage of at least one [unit], and I only lost one-half on job . . . one more plus attitude.

I find it very funny though that all of a sudden, even without realizing it, the guys themselves are thinking quality [and] good housekeeping and meaning it. Their concerns are slowly but ever so surely parallelling our own as managers.

[A manager] nervous. Me too. After twenty-six years, I'm seeing seventeen union people sitting with, not opposite [another supervisor] and foremen discussing *work allocations*. Mike as union rep is also nervous. As far as I'm concerned, *we make [plant] history*.

Finally a spin-off on line across from [Trim] zone. [Units] were again running off the ramp. But this time an employee phoned supervision not in zone and line was shut off. It would appear that our good people, which we have a number of, are no longer in fear or embarrassed of being called "suckholes," as we are all now in a common pot.

For the first time in twenty-six years I have seen, thirty seconds before the starting buzzer, *nine* people doing their jobs without notice or comment. I feel for the first time zone peer pressure. For example, "That guy doesn't fit. Why don't we get rid of him?"

One guy worked in another zone and was amazed at how little others care.

This was exactly the kind of cooperation management was looking for. For their part, workers appreciated several more tangible benefits. Trim became noticeably brighter and cleaner due to the combined efforts of managers and workers. More important, job training had begun on a voluntary basis, enabling the workers to rotate their jobs. They all felt this was helpful: even if later on they were to decide not to rotate jobs, the training itself was a welcome break from the monotony of the assembly line. There was a widespread sense that this just might be the beginning of a new kind of labor relations, one that might make coming to work less painful, and one that might hold the key to long-term job security.

QWL Expands

The pilot project in Trim grew slowly. Management expanded the size of the zone by bringing in eight new workers, all of whom agreed to take part in the project. Then, about a year after the pilot project began, management recalled about fifteen hundred laid-off workers. The recall provided the first easy opportunity for management to introduce QWL principles to a major part of the workforce. Even though there were as yet no specific plans for setting up QWL elsewhere in the plant, the company wanted the *idea* of QWL to become widespread among the workers.

In cooperation with the union, management gave all the recalled workers an eight-hour QWL orientation program. This included a motivational film with a message that one company executive later summed up this way: "If you don't get off your ass, you'll be out of business." Management then reinforced the message with a discussion of the financial problems faced by the company in a highly competitive international environment. The main emphasis was on the need for greater cooperation between labor and management.

The workers were also told about the QWL program in Trim and about other changes that the company had made or intended to make. Management tried to impress the recalled workers with the importance being given to quality and reported on such innovations as the "quality hotline," which enabled the workers to call a certain company telephone number to suggest improvements. Management promised that those who made suggestions would be contacted quickly, and that the workers would be consulted about the quality of the parts coming into the plant, about the status of the company's products in relation to those of its competitors, and about any proposed changes in product engineering and the design and location of jobs. The workers were also told that the plant environment was being improved through better housekeeping, better lighting, and repainting, and that oil spills and other safety hazards were receiving more attention.

After more than a year on layoff, most of the workers already had a fair idea that times were hard. Furthermore, some were already inclined to cooperate more actively with management because a joint union-management employee placement program had helped to place over a thousand laid-off workers in jobs outside the company.

During and after the QWL orientation, management moved production from one to two shifts. This was an enormously complex affair, involving a massive retraining program and the wholesale reallocation of jobs, but thanks largely to the atmosphere of goodwill created by the QWL orientation, the transition went very smoothly. After a week on the new system, according to management sources, average production was "way up." As one senior manager explained, "We did a super job there in getting them all worked up." As a sign of appreciation, management shut down the lines and put on a steak dinner for all 6,000 workers.

Meanwhile, although a second pilot project was to begin shortly in another part of the plant, Trim was still the only functioning QWL project. The zone had more than doubled in size, to about sixty workers on two shifts. Many of the original workers had left to take better jobs in other zones, and the remaining QWL veterans were spread thinly across both shifts. As a result, the pilot project had to start almost from scratch.

At a meeting of all the Trim workers, the chairperson of the project committee, together with the union and management members of the steering committee, spoke about the virtues of the project. They told the workers that QWL meant better treatment from management—that they would not be treated as "something lower than a supervisor." As before, few workers had a clear idea of what the program entailed. A member of the project committee reported later that a manager explained that QWL is "something you feel. You can't see it, you can't touch it, you have to want it." Managers told workers that since they, the workers, knew more about their jobs than management did, they should have more say about them. And management reminded them once again that the company was facing growing international competition, that both management and labor had to make common cause to save jobs. There was also some discussion of various worker-participation schemes in Japan and elsewhere. Finally, management encouraged the workers to talk about some of their ideas for improving their work and their working lives. The response was so eager that one worker, much impressed with the collective effort, exclaimed, "Boy, do we have this many ideas? It scares you!"

Nevertheless, some workers were still skeptical about such a vague program and felt that they had been through "too many snowjobs before." Some also felt that presenting QWL as a response to international competition implied that they were to blame for the company's problems, when instead they were "already doing their best." These reservations aside, however, most found the possibilities exciting and they overwhelmingly approved the expansion of the project.

A project committee was elected for each shift and a new

survey of workers' suggestions was made. The project committees selected job rotation as the top priority—perhaps because the workers had had less time to become habituated to their jobs—but other changes were also implemented. Although management refused to permit certain changes, including the removal of punch clocks and the immediate expansion of QWL to other zones, it did agree to make improvements in the ventilation system in the washroom, to repair a water fountain in the zone, to install picnic tables for the workers to eat on, and to pipe music into the work area. Several job-related improvements were also made: layout changes permitted better access to parts, better tools and cleaner work clothing were provided, and direct communication between workers and parts suppliers made stock inventories more reliable. There was also better access to the company's skilled trades personnel, so that machines and work stations could be maintained and repaired more efficiently; tool repair was also speeded up.

A more complex change involved the redistribution of work loads: those workers with more difficult jobs, or with jobs that required them to work more quickly to keep up with the line, got help, and it was agreed that time-standards personnel would not interfere with the changes. "We gained more balance between jobs, and the time gained wasn't taken away. It was our time," one worker reported. The extra seconds could be used to do a better job or to clean up the area. The company also promised that if the workers did not like the new distribution of work, they could change back.

Management had already promised the project committee that, except under specified circumstances, the total work load and number of jobs in the zone would not be changed until new product models were introduced. Some workers came to regard this as a significant concession, although others felt that "when the company agreed not to increase work loads, they made sure work loads were already heavy." Management, however, denied that jobs had been sped up in advance.

The most difficult problem for the project committees was the setting up of a relaxation area for the zone. Although the area had been approved by the steering committee and was consistent with the goal of enhancing the workers' sense of identity with the zone, the company refused to implement it, partly because of major disagreements over what a relaxation area should contain. Some workers thought it should be constructed on a rather grand scale, similar to those they had learned about from company materials concerning QWL in Japanese factories. Management, on the other hand, wanted something cheaper and more modest. The result was an impasse.

On the whole, and despite such unresolved issues, the workers' attitude toward management remained positive. This was especially evident with those workers in Trim who came into frequent contact with managers while serving on the project committees. "You get to know your supervisor and general foreman better," one committee member reported. "It's different from knowing them in the plant. You see the pressures the supervisors are under." In these meetings the supervisors "got complaints off their chest." Supervisors explained the kinds of pressure they were under from management further up the ladder, which led to a certain amount of personal sympathy for them. It became fairly common to see the supervisors and the workers eating together, something that had been exceedingly rare before.

In addition to promoting sympathy for supervisors, the project made some workers feel they were actually superior to their immediate bosses. This was apparent on the second shift in Trim (not the shift with the model "human relations" supervisor) when senior managers asked the workers to evaluate their supervisor's competence. "I'm holding a gun to his head," a plant manager assured them when they complained that the supervisor was not performing well enough. Some of the workers then ordered the supervisor to improve—or else.

In these ways the program began to change the relationship between workers and supervisors. Some workers no longer saw management as management, either because they saw their supervisor as a friend or because they considered him to be below them in the corporate hierarchy. One senior manager who helped to implement the QWL program reported that he was often given pieces of information by workers who said they were not "for management's ears." He approved, and said it showed that the workers no longer regarded him as management. Thanks to QWL, the workers' sense of the line dividing them from management had been blurred.

This is where the QWL project in Trim stood at the end of its second year. Although only a limited amount had been accomplished, it was nevertheless judged a moderate success by both management and workers. This contrasted dramatically with the only other pilot project in the plant, which had been established shortly after the plant went on two shifts.

The Short Unhappy Life of the Experiment in the Paint Zone

The steering committee chose the Paint Zone, an area with about seventy spray painters on two shifts, for the second pilot project. The zone had several favorable features. For one, even though many of the workers had only recently returned from layoff, they already had a strong sense of group identity. They all did the same job and took pride in their unique skills—skills that, unlike those of most "semi-skilled" auto workers—were well paid outside the plant as well. Their sense of group identity was also fostered by the fact that they all worked together in a large booth, a well-defined structure that set them apart form the rest of the plant.

Another reason the steering committee selected Paint was the very visible nature of its workers' contribution to the finished product: paint defects, such as bubbles and overspray, are difficult to hide from consumers. In addition, although this zone is organized around a subassembly line that is separate from the main line, work in many other parts of the plant is highly sensitive to interruptions in the flow of work from Paint. As a result, management was especially concerned that labor relations in this zone be harmonious. A final factor was the considerable influence that two of the members of the steering committee had in the zone.

On the other side of the balance sheet, Paint had one serious drawback: "bad" labor relations. The zone had always been one of the most militant and the workers' resistance against hard-line supervisors had been relatively successful. Consequently, management saw the successful diffusion of QWL into Paint as a true test of its potential to reduce the resistance of workers elsewhere.

The spray painters were introduced to QWL in much the same way the workers in Trim had been. By this time, however, the consultants' role was less central, so that most of the orientation was conducted by union and management personnel and by a member of one of the project committees in Trim.

As in Trim, the workers in Paint were generally receptive. This was reinforced when management agreed on the spot to pay them for the hours that are scheduled at the beginning of the shift, even if work hours were reduced later. This removed a major and long-standing irritant. In the resulting aura of enthusiasm the workers elected two project committees—one for each shift. As one worker recalled, "The guys really wanted to experiment. They felt this was the first time they weren't going to be dictated to."

The project got off to a good start. Many of the workers appreciated the fact that company executives went out of their way to build up a friendly rapport with them. This was especially true of the project committee members, who began to feel that they had closer relations with their supervisors' superiors than the supervisors had. This feeling of being more powerful and influential than the supervisors was strengthened when the plant manager allowed the workers on one shift in Paint to select their own supervisor. One worker was even temporarily put in charge of production quality in the zone.

Management taught the project committees the few elementary techniques in problem-solving that are common in QWL programs (for instance, brainstorming, the listing of causes of production problems, the use of bar graphs and simple cost-benefit analysis). Members of the project committee then distributed questionnaires in the zone, asking the workers to propose improvements. All the respondents reaffirmed their support for the project, and made numerous suggestions. These included an enclosed eating area, a free pair of work boots each year, personal coveralls, a new water fountain and a new emergency eyewash station, better tools and better training in tool maintenance, job rotation, more spacious work areas, better showers, better ventilation to remove fumes form the area, and stereo music systems (this last request arose because head masks and other protective equipment precluded the use of earphones). The two committees then set priorities among these suggestions, based on the breadth of their appeal, their importance to the workers, and the likelihood of their being implemented. Eventually the enclosed eating area was given top priority.

The frustrations were immediate. Not only was the company reluctant to implement the eating area project because it was so costly, but it balked at most of the other suggestions as well. One of the project committees gave management an ultimatum: agree to improvements or "It's back to the old days; it's war like before. You're just trying to keep us quiet." At another point the workers threatened to hold a sit-down strike. This discontent remained even after a small improvement—a new system for distributing coveralls—was made, largely because by this time some workers were convinced that the belated concession was more the result of their threats than of the QWL project. Even this taste of victory turned sour when it was learned, to the apparent surprise of management as well as workers, that it might mean a loss of work for the person who distributed the coveralls. Several workers were also angered when they learned that they would be charged if they lost the keys to the storage lockers for their new coveralls.

One other improvement was made, however, and although it did not offset the workers' overall sense of disappointment, it did give them the sense that they were not being completely ignored. Management consulted one of the project committees about the choice of a new supervisor for the zone. The workers generally got along well with the new choice, and he was praised for being willing to "bend over backward to solve problems."

Aside from this improvement, the other changes that were made were few and minor. Better tools were provided, but this had not been a high priority. Management also donated a top for the zone's garbage can, a top that nevertheless failed to keep away the fruit flies!

Not surprisingly, the workers' initial enthusiasm for the project quickly waned. In addition, it was clear that a major obstacle had emerged: top management was no longer backing the project. Senior managers saw it as time-consuming and expensive, and thought it was not leading to any meaningful improvement in labor relations. A senior executive claimed that because the project committees were being paid overtime for meeting after work, and because of other costs, the company would have "gone bankrupt" if the projects had been diffused across the plant. Top plant management was also having difficulty gaining genuine support from either middle management or the front-line supervisors, who were understandably concerned that the projects would undermine their authority. The more the project committees asked for, the less management was willing to grant. Management members on the steering committee simply vetoed the proposals and the honeymoon between the union and the company drew to a close.

No doubt the honeymoon would have been over sooner if it had been widely known that the project in Trim had caused the elimination of four jobs in an adjacent area. This was of course contrary to the gentleman's agreement with management that QWL would not lead to job loss. Other jobs were lost in conjunction with technological changes, especially robotics, whose acceptance was facilitated by QWL, but no records were kept. The speed of the line had also increased—from 48 to 65 units an hour—since QWL had come to Progress.

Finally, about four months after the project in Paint began, the steering committee stopped meeting altogether, in part because the union representatives refused to attend. One project committee member in Paint remembered waiting for over three months without hearing from the steering committee about the latest proposals for improvements. He became frustrated that management "wouldn't go along with things that cost money" and that the workers were unable to get "anything solid like music in the booths." Project committee members concluded that the QWL experiment was a "big screw-up" because management "passed the buck" on too many decisions.

Eventually a union representative on the steering committee recommended that project committee meetings be suspended until management showed a greater interest in the project. One of the project committees in Paint then decided to disband, and could not be dissuaded by the QWL consultants and management personnel. The decision was generally supported by the workers in the zone.

In defiance of the union members on the steering committee, the second project committee in Paint continued to limp along, despite criticism from the workers that the meetings were not accomplishing much. It was at this time that an emergency eyewash stand, which had been on order for some time, was installed in the zone. This did little to salvage the project, however, partly because the workers felt it was a measure that should have been implemented long before through the union-management health-and-safety committee.

After a while it became clear to everyone that further improvements were not being made, and without the steering committee meeting to oversee the project, management too gave up. A senior manager later called the program in Paint a "give away," and argued that the company could have spent "a billion dollars" and never satisfied the workers there. With growing opposition from union leaders, with continuing lack of support from middle management, and with long and potentially con-flict-ridden negotiations for a new collective bargaining agree-ment due, it would have taken a miracle for the project to continue.

So it was that less than a year after the project had been extended into Paint, it came to a halt. In over two years, fewer than 150 out of 6,000 workers had become involved. Yet QWL was far from dead. In its next incarnation it would take on a dramatically different form—and this time it would be done without the union.

The Quality Booster Program

Several months after the demise of the steering committee, the union began collective bargaining over the next contract. The union negotiators brought with them a long list of proposals for reforming the QWL program, but they were not a priority. For one thing, by this time QWL had become the center of a major political controversy in the local, which will be discussed in the next section. In addition, some of management's contract demands were a direct threat to the union and were the focus of union attention. Management called for a reduction in the number of stewards, a change that would have weakened the leadership's links to the membership. Management also de-manded a division of the membership into two seniority lists, an explosive proposition that, if implemented, would have split the membership in two. Both proposals were recognized as an undisguised attempt to divide and rule. It was in this context that the union members of the steering committee officially decided to put the QWL projects "on the back burner," a place they had unofficially occupied for some months.

By this point cooperation between workers and management had become an entrenched process, however, one that went far beyond what had originally been agreed to by the union. In the previous two years, management had instituted a number of innovations that were part of an overall "human relations" approach, which stressed the value of a less overtly authoritarian style of management as a way of improving worker motivation and hence productivity. The company systematically trained supervisors across the plant in "cooperative supervision," one of the new industrial relations techniques being introduced to replace the previous "adversarial" supervisory style. In the new situation, supervisors were far less prone to shout at workers and were more likely to settle disputes informally without the union's being called in. As a result, the stewards filed very few grievances.

High rates of unemployment and continuing fears about job security in the plant helped this process along. Supervisors had far fewer problems with absenteeism. The rate of absenteeism fell so low, one worker observed, that "right now, the company doesn't care if you take a day off." In this way the workers' sense of vulnerability and management's human relation approach operated in tandem—the one by fear, the other by seduction— to foster what had become a much broader QWL agenda.

By this time some workers were participating in exchange visits with workers in other plants owned by the same company in order to discuss quality problems, while others were consulting with the representatives of companies supplying parts to the plant, and still others were discussing changes in product quality with auto dealers. Workers were also consulting individually with management about changes in model design and about the organization of work as it affected their jobs. At times, management even broke the traditional taboo against stopping the assembly lines in the midst of production so that workers and supervisors could discuss these and other matters. Management had also made it a policy to send greeting cards to each worker at Christmas and explanatory letters whenever there were major production changes in the plant. During special visitation days management took workers' families on tours of the plant.

All this occurred at a time when the workers were receiving

unprecedented attention from outside the plant as well. Using workers as the actors, Progress Motors had for some time been showing television commercials based on the theme that the workers' pride in their jobs was leading to major improvements in the quality of the plant's automobiles. This theme was reinforced in numerous newspaper articles and in television documentaries about the plant's improved labor relations and working environment.

These changes, which management dubbed "employee communication activities" or "employee involvement activities," set the stage for the most important of all the company's broader QWL initiatives. This was what management called the "quality booster program." At its heart was a new job, called a "quality booster." (Because this job fit into an old job classification, it did not require a re-negotiation of the contract.) The quality booster was a production worker who had the unusual responsibility of policing the work of a group of eight or ten of his fellow workers. This involved two supervisory functions: first, ensuring the repair of defective units before they were moved out of the zone, and second, investigating the reasons the defect had occurred in the first place. The booster had a degree of discretionary authority that was previously unheard of among production workers. He had an exceptionally broad mandate to investigate the reasons for poor work and was even empowered to shut down the line if too many defective products were leaving the area. Beyond this, the booster was supposed to encourage his fellow workers to do better work, and to relieve the supervisor of responsibilities most directly related to job performance. With the booster acting as the center of communication both with workers in the area and with management, front-line supervisors could, it was hoped, devote more time to overall planning and administration.

In effect, the boosters were a new first line of supervision, but cheaper: although their pay rate was marginally higher than the rates for most production workers, this was far less than a supervisor's salary. There was another important difference between boosters and front-line supervisors: the booster had no authority to discipline the workers and was thus inclined, both as a member of a work group and by the logic of his position, to adopt a human relations style, which emphasized cooperation rather than coercion in order to get the work done. Such, at least, was management's intention.

The booster program was also designed to solve a related supervisory problem. For many years the company had been trying to find enough supervisors who were "doers"—people who would take on the "donkey work" of rushing from worker to worker with a tool replacement, a pair of coveralls that fit, a new work glove; of showing a new worker the ropes; of cleaning up an oil spill—all the minutiae that need constant attention. Often such donkey work requires front-line supervisors to become actively involved in workers' jobs (even though the collective bargaining agreement expressly forbids this). But few supervisors know the jobs well enough to do them efficiently, largely because they do not have access to the hidden knowledge and skills that the workers have, while workers who have that knowledge are generally unwilling to become supervisors, partly because of the enormous pressures that go with the job. The booster program was one method for management to get around such headaches. If the boosters could do the detailed donkey work, they would pave the way for a new human relations style of supervisor who did not have to use bully-boy tactics and the old "two-by-four method" to get work done; supervisors could then play "good guy" while keeping their shirts white and hands clean.

Management did not have total control over the choice of boosters, since this was to a certain extent determined by seniority provisions in the union contract. However, management was able to encourage those workers it considered to be "spokesmen" and "leaders" to apply for the booster positions.

Meanwhile, workers considered less suitable were discouraged from applying. At the same time, the company embarked upon an ambitious training program for boosters, which taught them how to do the job using some of the motivational theories that were becoming standard fare for the plant's supervisors. All this lent them a status that was somewhat above most other workers, and helped to condition them psychologically to jobs that were highly ambiguous.

According to management, the boosters had to be "natural leaders": they had to have considerable seniority and the self-confidence to take on such a job in the first place. They also tended to be the same kinds of workers as those involved in the project committees, and indeed several had been active in those committees in Trim and Paint. It was also significant that, in earlier years and under a different management regime, some of the boosters had been leading militants. As one union steward observed, "A lot of workers who had been militant became more concerned about quality." Thanks to anxieties about job security and the opportunities presented by the booster program, informal plant-floor leadership took on a pro-management orientation.

The key point about the booster program was that it had the potential for turning much of the supervision of workers into self-supervision. Work-group identity, which at one time implied a group solidarity based on resistance to management power, was now expected to revolve around cooperation with management. From management's point of view, the booster program had the same goal as the original QWL pilot projects: a more cooperative relationship between labor and management as a means to greater productivity, with product quality as a key element. Moreover, it had the potential for reaching this goal without depending on union support, with its unpredictable political ups and downs. Furthermore, because the booster program promised less to workers, it also ran less risk of failure. Most important, however, was the speed with which the program could be diffused. Whereas the pilot QWL projects were snails that took almost three years to crawl along a tortuous path, the booster program took off across the entire plant with one great leap, and while the pilot projects eventually involved at the most only 150 workers, the booster program recruited and trained 150 boosters and placed them in nearly every department *in less than four months*. Since each booster worked with eight to ten workers, this meant that in one way or another approximately fifteen hundred quickly became part of the program. Thus it was the booster program that marked the beginning of QWL as a plantwide set of labor-management relations that went far beyond the confines of the kind of QWL defined by the original pilot projects.

The Union Withdraws but QWL Continues

As noted earlier, even after the steering committee disbanded, QWL as an official program of union-management collaboration (the projects in Paint and Trim) was the center of heated controversy in the union. The four local leaders who served on the steering committee bore the brunt of mounting criticism, and it eventually became clear that an overwhelming majority of the membership and the local leadership were opposed to this kind of cooperation. At a general membership meeting, a strong majority voted to withdraw from the official QWL program.

Since the pilot projects had been defunct for some time, this decision to pull out was in one sense irrelevant. It was irrelevant in a broader and more important sense as well: QWL had long since become a quite different and much larger process than the carefully defined projects in Trim and Paint, so the union was not really pulling out of QWL at all. Indeed it could not, since management had assumed transparent control of that larger process with the quality booster program.

By this time, many workers and union leaders sensed the danger and opposed this process, but there was little they could do. The process now had supporters on the plant floor, especially among the often highly influential boosters. Regardless of union policy, management at Progress remained committed to its own version of QWL, a "softer" style of industrial relations that had already reached right into the work groups, crossing the adversarial line separating the workers from their immediate superiors.

The future of QWL at Progress Motors is anybody's guess. What is clear, however, is that it was far more difficult for the union to keep a handle on QWL than it had first thought. "How could we lose?" a local union leader had asked rhetorically when the steering committee was first being set up. Hindsight provided the answer.

Conclusion

The most striking characteristic of the rise of QWL at Progress Motors was its constant belittling in practice of what it claimed to be in theory. Contrary to the most rudimentary principles of democracy, QWL was a consistently top-down affair. The few in the offices at the top decided the general policies and specific changes for the many on the plant floor below. In fact, the more the workers became involved in QWL, the less they had to say about its implementation.

The QWL program started out as the creation of two decision-making hierarchies, one an apparent center of power, the other a real one. It gave prominent roles to top plant managers and union leaders, and, less formally, to those somewhat shadowy servants of power, the QWL consultants. These few agreed to a decision-making structure that was supposedly designed to give them control over the way the program evolved. This control was formally vested in the veto power that the steering committee had over any initiative that filtered up through the project committees.

In a fundamental sense, however, the fate of QWL was not determined by the seemingly all-powerful steering committee at all. Instead, *real* power resided in the executive suite. That the steering committee had many of the trappings but little of the substance of power is clear in retrospect. The most important changes in industrial relations—including the numerous human relations innovations and the quality booster program—occurred off to one side of the steering committee's activities. These changes spread throughout the plant with great speed, yet neither the workers nor their union representatives have any influence over where QWL is to go from here. Only management has the power of *initiative* in the QWL process. Only management has the power to *implement* QWL. And only management has the necessary resources—time, money, and expertise—for shaping the development of QWL. All of this had been true from the start. Yet its importance had been hidden from the workers by their fear of unemployment, by their trust in individual managers and consultants, and by their hope that management's power would be put to new, genuinely cooperative uses. Now that the significance of management power was once again clear, so much had changed—including the shape of QWL.

3

The QWL Experiments at Universal Electric

In this chapter we turn to a second, quite common, kind of QWL program, but one that is very different from that introduced at Progress Motors. This program was instituted in a large electronics plant owned by Universal Electric, a pseudonym for one of the giant American multinationals in the industry. The plant comprises a jumble of cement and red brick buildings with windows so dirty that the sun cannot pass through. This jumble mirrors the organization of work: unlike the auto plant at Universal Electric, there is no core labor process, such as the assembly line, to give production an overall uniformity and coherent pattern. Instead, jobs and working conditions vary enormously from building to building and from department to department. While in some departments workers stand in front of individual machines, in other departments groups of workers sit at workbenches and in still others they work at assembly lines; in many departments there is a mix. Pay varies too: some work at fixed hourly wages, while some work for piece rates; some also get production bonuses. These and other differences reflect the variety of the plant's products, which include traffic lights, telephone equipment, radio components, fluorescent lighting, electrical transformers, a wide variety of chemical products, and much else.

For almost ten years the outlook for job security at Universal Electric has been bleak for everyone. Since the late 1970s, entire product lines have been reduced, eliminated, or sold off. Between 1981 and 1983 well over half the jobs were lost and many more had been lost before that. The few hundred workers who remained had on average about twenty-five years service apiece. Some were only working part time and all were anxious about the security of their jobs. In contrast to the mood in the car plant, where concern about job security was mixed with optimism, many at Universal Electric had given up any hope that their jobs could be saved.

For all these differences, there are nevertheless basic similarities between the two workplaces. First, QWL in both plants was shaped by management's preoccupation with profit and by the workers' concern about job security; and second, in both places there was a long history of hostility between bosses and workers. It took a bloody battle to bring a production workers' union into Universal Electric in the first place. This bad beginning set the climate for subsequent labor relations, and work stoppages have formed a major part of the plant's subsequent history. A Universal executive contended that until recently the union "could run this plant up and down as they saw fit," a claim that union leaders saw as only partly exaggerating the degree of solidarity and militancy characteristic of the plant. Another manager alleged that work stoppages were "so well orchestrated that if workers [in one area] left at 1 o'clock, ten seconds later workers [in other areas] would leave. They had a very good communications network."

For many years, until the mid-1970s, management had not been seriously concerned about these stoppages. "They weren't costing us much," a member of management explained, "because business was so good." For the most part management relied on (relatively) high wages and (relatively) harsh penalties to maintain an adequate level of control. Management felt this was a tolerable degree of conflict.

But about ten years ago the profit margins that sustained this tolerance began to narrow. Universal became concerned that the plant's overhead was often higher than that of its competitors, which were becoming increasingly aggressive. Several of the plant's products were also facing volatile shifts in demand. Management therefore embarked on a policy of cutting costs by using short-term layoffs and recalls to adjust the size of the workforce to immediate needs. The result was that, as one executive put it, the plant had "a terrible goddamn name." A "real credibility gap" emerged, with Universal blaming the workers for wage demands that it considered out of line with productivity, and the workers blaming Universal for not making the investment needed to keep the plant competitive. Work stoppages were especially common around the issue of layoffs, and both stoppages and layoffs usually came without warning. Meanwhile, grievances had backed up far past the point where the contract-mandated procedure was effective. As one worker put it, labor-management relations were "the pits."

At this point, losses had reached the point where hard decisions had to be made: the cost of conflict was no longer tolerable to management. Faced with shrinking revenues, the company sold off pieces of the plant, introduced a new chain of command, and shifted many managers around. Management also took a get-tough line with the union leadership. When this proved ineffective, senior Universal executives took a new tack—enter QWL.

In the late 1960s Universal had attempted to convince the workers of the need to "work together to give our customer his money's worth." Many workers found this appeal for cooperation unconvincing, and one manager admitted that, until well into the current crisis, management was only "paying lip-service to quality of working life." Once it became clear that hard-line techniques for improving productivity had failed, however, management began to take QWL more seriously. There were reasons for this: first, the crisis itself; second, the arrival of a management team that was committed to QWL as a method for cutting supervisory costs and increasing worker productivity. One very influential manager was convinced of the need for QWL because of his experiences elsewhere. A mentor had advised him in the following vein: "Don't think that engineers know what they're doing. The worker on the floor knows more about the machine. So, what you should do when there's a problem is to get all the workers together and get them to solve the problem." Traditional controls on workers were old hat: "The workers know the shortcuts, they know how it works. In effect, they have mastered it. The methods men are trained to set up the jobs for the average worker and there's no such thing." Workers who were committed to the company could be expected to produce at levels way above the average.

This is why, after years of forcing workers to fit into general work rules and to produce to fixed targets, management at Universal, as at Progress Motors, became interested in moving past the frontier of control that had marked the previous boundaries of worker productivity. This is why management began to consult with outside experts about the various QWL options. Eventually, in 1981, one management consulting firm was told to go ahead and set up an experimental QWL project in the plant.

Once Again, Design from Above

Unlike their counterparts at Progress Motors, management at Universal Electric decided to implement a QWL program that centered on a very specific "problem-solving" method. The structure of the QWL groups themselves was also to be different: they were composed of individual workers rather than worker representatives.

Management had great hopes for this new approach to labor relations. The QWL consultant who had been hired by the company to start the program explained that the scheme had a broader purpose: to "convey to employees that their role is changing." As he put it, "We have to communicate that productivity is more than working harder. It is getting the employee involved in other aspects of productivity." He argued that management could expect an "increased efficiency in the use of resources, reflected, for example, in quality and methods improvements, and in cost reductions." He also promised that there would be "an improved quality of work life, demonstrated by reduced absenteeism, fewer grievances, and increased job satisfaction." More generally, he saw the process as leading to the "creation of a vehicle for management-labor cooperation and consultation."

The core of the program, called "cooperative decision-making," or CDM, consisted of an integrated set of problem-solving techniques that were taught to a small number of workers organized into a CDM group. These groups were taught how to choose a production-related problem from their own work environment according to such criteria as: Can we solve this problem? Is there enough authority, knowledge, and influence in the group to solve it? Are there rules or laws that limit us? Next, the group was taught to solve each problem according to a specific set of steps. These included defining the root causes of the problem, analyzing its aspects, listing and testing a variety of solutions, implementing the preferred solution, and, finally, evaluating the results. On the ground that workers would not normally possess the relevant expertise for solving these problems, the CDM groups were assisted in their deliberations by salaried "resource people" from sales, engineering, finance, and other departments. Unlike the production workers, who came to the CDM groups on a voluntary basis, the resource personnel—if they did not volunteer—were ordered to join the group by their superiors.

Once it had decided to implement a cooperative decision-making project, senior plant management selected the area where it was to begin. It chose the transformer department, an ancient and cluttered area of the plant where approximately forty men and women stood or sat at individual workbenches assembling electronic components.

As in the case of the selection of Trim at Progress Motors, management chose the Transformer Department primarily because the workers and supervisors in the area already enjoyed relatively harmonious relations, thanks partly to the presence of an "employee-centered" supervisor. With only about forty workers, the department was also "easy to get your arms around," one manager explained. In addition, a successful CDM project in the Transformer Department would help change the workers' perception—which was accurate—that the department had a low place in management's overall priorities. Management also thought that there were a number of problems in the zone that workers could resolve without too much difficulty.

All of these reasons made the Transformer Department a good starting point for CDM. Success there would provide an attractive "demonstration effect," so that workers in other areas would want CDM groups of their own. On the other hand, if the CDM project in the Transformer Department were to fail, this would not have an adverse effect on other areas of the plant because the department was isolated, having few connections with other aspects of production. From management's point of view, the Transformer Department was thus a good bet and a "relatively safe area for a QWL experiment."

It was not until management had made this major decision that the workers were approached. The QWL consultant then conducted two day-long sessions with the workers in the department and with salaried personnel in the plant's offices. He outlined CDM in order to do "a lot of climate-setting," as one Universal executive described it. The consultant asked both salaried and hourly workers to identify the major problems facing the plant. This request elicited very similar lists of problems, indicating the existence of a great many common concerns.

Management then told the workers in the Transformer Department that the economic situation meant that it had two choices: bring in outside management to decide the plant's fate, or ask the workers (together with management) to help determine the future of the plant. As one worker translated this choice, it meant "either improve or go out the door." Implied threat aside, the invitation to cooperate made sense to many workers since, as one observed, "the employees who work on the job have a lot of knowledge, so they can solve the problem with the cooperation of management." The vast majority of the workers in the department decided to give the QWL scheme a try. This was almost a foregone conclusion: "The intact nature of [the department], the threat of closing down, and the confidence in the people communicated by the new manager all contributed to people being willing to volunteer for the attempt," one company executive reported.

The union representing the production workers at Universal was not willing to cooperate, however. The national leadership officially opposed QWL as a scheme to co-opt workers for management's ends. Although management reported that some of the senior leaders of the union local were not opposed to the project, the influence of the national meant that the project had at best only the "tacit support" or "passive opposition" of the local. For their part, local union leaders claim to have opposed QWL strenuously.

Management did not regard this opposition from the union as an insurmountable obstacle. For one thing, influential union activists in the Transformer Department were behind the project. For another, there was enthusiastic support for the project among influential leaders in the union that represented the majority of the plant's office workers. While there was some management concern that the CDM project might be used as a "political tool" by the production workers' union, others hoped that those workers involved in a successful project would use it as a "spring-board to union office."

QWL in One Department

Despite their union's opposition, then, most of the workers in the Transformer Department readily agreed to try the CDM problem-solving methods and began a five-week training session. They met once a week, but although they got a break from their jobs and received full pay, most were frustrated to find that many of the techniques for solving problems were too abstract and hard to apply to their own work situations. Nevertheless, management deemed the program a success, and at the end of the training period assigned the Transformer workers to four CDM teams, each composed of workers who did the same job. The job was to become the basis of team identity.

Management also arranged for volunteers to serve as team coordinators. The local president of the office workers' union volunteered, as did three hourly workers from the Transformer Department, all active trade unionists (two were stewards). All four were given an additional forty hours of training in CDM techniques and then sent back to lead the groups.

Most of the workers began to participate in CDM meetings with considerable enthusiasm. They identified numerous problems and used CDM selection criteria to choose production-related difficulties to work on. The next step was to apply the CDM problem-solving techniques.

At first management was also very enthusiastic about the progress the teams were making, but as time went on it was disappointed to find that, despite the training, the teams were not able to operate effectively. It turned out that neither the team members nor the coordinators had a sufficient grasp of the CDM principles and techniques to solve real problems. Furthermore, numerous doubts began to emerge about the usefulness of CDM problem-solving: many of the problems the workers chose seemed far too difficult and complex to be solved by the teams. In addition, the coordinators were resented by some of the team members because they were "selling" CDM instead of teaching it. There was also criticism of the extra pay the coordinators received (an additional $15 an hour, four hours a week). When a few assertive individuals moved into this vacuum of authority and confidence, undermining the coordinators even further and threatening to dominate decision-making, the problem seemed insurmountable.

The resource people with skills in engineering, accounting, and so on were especially prone to view the tightly structured CDM problem-solving procedure as "for the birds." "I mean, why go through all this guff when there is either no solution or else there is a solution that's just obvious?" one engineer asked.

This same engineer recalled a work-flow problem his team had grappled with for a long time before giving up: it would have required the redesign of the whole production process before any improvements could have been achieved, and this was far beyond the scope of CDM. Another CDM team worked for several weeks on a different work-flow problem. The engineer laughed at how the problem had been suddenly solved when one of the workers shifted a box that stood between her and the parts she was assembling.

Team morale deteriorated further when more and more workers found that there was no "quick fix" for some of the problems they were supposed to solve. In addition, many team members concluded that those problems that could be tackled did not need CDM techniques. Discontent mounted and workers began to drop out of the teams.

After six months the teams were so depleted that management decided to intervene. The immediate impetus was a "disaster" of a retraining session, run by the outside consultant, which had further undermined the team coordinators' already shaky sense of confidence in CDM and in themselves. Management now took charge. In order to salvage the program, it called a meeting to discuss the problems the teams were facing. It then unilaterally introduced two major changes. The first was a change in the basic CDM framework: some of the emphasis on complex techniques for problem-solving was withdrawn. (The more complex techniques took so long to learn, one worker observed, that "by that time you'd be retired.") In their place came a new emphasis on "job analysis," a set of rather rudimentary methods. Most of these were taken from the fundamentals of "Job Instruction Training," a formula for training new employees (practiced by corporations since the 1920s) that involves breaking down each job into its components, mastering each component separately, putting all the components back together, and then doing each job, once again, as a whole. Many workers found this method easier to master, partly because, by being so practical and familiar, it offset the abstractness of the original CDM techniques for problem-solving.

Because the new methods focused almost exclusively on the sequence of production, workers got a better sense of how jobs were done throughout the department. By showing workers the connection between their own jobs and those of their fellow workers, the revised CDM framework made it easier for them to identify with other workers, and reinforced their identification with the product as a whole. "That's when CDM really became productive," one management member said, "because it's a process function and they could see their jobs impact way down on somebody else."

The changes in the CDM framework also made it easier for the coordinators to do their jobs. They were able to teach the new method to the groups, and this helped them regain confidence and improve their relations with the teams. This in turn made it more difficult for strong-willed individuals to dominate the groups.

The second major change management imposed was in the composition of the groups. From now on each team was to be made up of workers who did a variety of different jobs in the Transformer Department: the teams were to have a broad perspective on the work process in order to properly understand and solve problems. In effect, management's new policy was to sacrifice a certain amount of smaller scale work-group identity and job identity in order to instill a greater sense of *departmental* identity.

In response to the vulnerability felt by the coordinators, management also set up a review committee, which was given final approval of the decisions made by the teams. But since management had final authority over the *implementation* of the decisions, this change was a "sham from the beginning," as one plant executive noted. The committee's function was to serve as a "security blanket" for the coordinators. "They insisted that it be formal," he continued. "They had no idea how far they could go. To an hourly employee, the foreman is most important and there is awe for those above." So the review committee, made up of a few senior managers, became a sounding board for coordinators who wanted upper management to assure them that front-line and middle management would cooperate with their decisions.

Senior plant managers believed that these changes—particularly the revised CDM format—were responsible for the increase in productivity that occurred at this time. Although data measuring this increase were lacking, the productivity boost was held to have been a healthy one, more than adequate to compensate for the CDM training costs.

According to an attitudinal survey conducted by management after these changes had been introduced in the Transformer Department, most of the production workers still involved with the program were reasonably satisfied. A closer look at the results, however, revealed that much of this satisfaction derived from their greater opportunity to get to know their fellow workers, rather than from any changes in their jobs. Beyond this, the survey indicated widespread apathy brought on by boring meetings and an inadequate sense of direction in the groups. Above all, there was no sense of accomplishment.

It was not until a full year after CDM began at Universal Electric that a proposed solution to a straightforward production problem reached the review committee. At this point, however, ongoing layoffs had led to a high turnover in the Transformer Department, as more senior workers from other areas bumped out CDM team members. The new entrants had not been trained in CDM techniques and were less inclined to cooperate, especially since many had unpleasant memories of authoritarian management elsewhere in the plant. Despite this, or perhaps because of it, some veteran CDM members remained convinced that taking part in CDM was the best response to job insecurity. "We're all in it for one thing," one team member said. "We need the job, so we've got to get this place going."

The teams continued to meet, and solutions to various production problems slowly began to take shape. Many of the problems, however—such as the best location for a sorting tray or enlargement of an oil drum to reduce spills—were petty, and sometimes there was the added frustration of a long delay in implementing a proposed solution. Management would veto the solution, or a supervisor would block it, or a lack of resources would interfere with its installation.

As in the auto plant, so too in the electronics plant, the introduction of QWL began slowly and proceeded slowly—too slowly to be considered a success in light of the promises that gave it birth.

Some Innovations in Human Relations

Management's efforts to get workers and supervisors to cooperate soon went far beyond the original QWL program. Once again, much of this expansion was in the area of "human relations." "Engineers started going down to the floor," a senior plant executive recalled. "The section manager would go down on the floor. I would go down to them [the workers], talk to them, listen to their problems. I still do." Management's social work on the shop floor was not, by and large, an attempt at forming genuinely decent relationships with the workers. Instead, these same executives who smilingly glad-handed the production workers referred to them in private as "stupid" and "illiterate." Several of the senior managers were particularly contemptuous toward female workers, especially the older ones, calling them "old cows" and "stupid cows." Perhaps this was because, although women were almost entirely absent from union leadership positions, quite a few of the most seasoned and toughest militants in the plant were women.

These often hypocritical efforts at improving rapport between workers and middle- and upper-level management were complemented by attempts to lessen anxiety about layoffs. Management tried to limit the amount of "bouncing people around," and paid special attention to long-time employees. Workers who reached twenty-five years of service not only received the normal plaque and pin, but were taken out to an expensive restaurant. Female workers were given corsages to mark their twenty-fifth and fortieth years with the company, or their retirement. Universal also agreed to provide retraining for a few long-time employees who were to be laid off due to the shutting down of production in certain departments. All workers were given more tools and work clothing (each worker was given three work smocks). Management introduced other innovations directed specifically at the CDM teams. For example, as compensation for the contributions of team members and because they had declined payment for the savings resulting from the problems they solved, management hosted an annual dinner for all the teams.

Meanwhile, however, discontent began to emerge among front-line and middle-level management. Several lower- and middle-level managers saw the suggestions coming from the CDM teams as a threat to their jobs. To a certain extent this was true. Senior plant managers argued that the company's traditional suggestion-box program had failed because lower and middle management had blocked good suggestions for fear they would lead to intrusions into their own jurisdictions. Now that the CDM teams were taking the place of the suggestion boxes, these supervisors, engineers, and managers were being circumvented and their discontent was growing. Top plant management therefore made it a policy to pay more attention to the middle and lower levels of their own ranks. Prior to the beginning of the QWL program, most supervisors had been ignored by management. More than a few felt that for years they had been treated as "whipping boys"; now they too were asked to explain their problems and to offer suggestions for resolving them.

In addition, training courses were set up for supervisors. They were introduced to B. F. Skinner's behaviorist psychology and to some of its applications in motivating workers. They were taught "constructive discipline," which included learning to "level and listen" to workers in order to understand their problems better and counsel them more effectively. They learned about "autocratic" and "democratic" styles of supervision by playing roles as both workers and supervisors in simulated shop-floor situations. Eventually they learned a "catalytic" style of supervision that used both methods, and gave them a broader repertoire of ways to motivate workers. Some supervisors were given training so that they would be able to move up the management ladder. Senior management hoped that this might counter the poor morale associated with being "stuck" at the bottom of the hierarchy.

These human relations innovations were directed more toward discontent in management's ranks than toward the workers' problems. They were not a source of real change in the work lives of either supervisors or middle managers. "I'm not saying we made any great change in [the supervisors'] behavior," a manager closely associated with these training programs admitted, but the changes still "made them feel important."

These innovations had less impact on supervisory practices than similar changes had had at Progress Motors, largely because the supervisors at Universal had always enjoyed more discretion in the handling of conflict—issues were more likely to be settled informally than through the grievance procedure. (At the same time, supervisors at Universal were not dissuaded from using the procedure, since management regarded it as a "safety valve." No grievances were a signal to plant managers that a supervisor was a "sweetheart" or that he was too intimidating, which might lead to an "explosion.")

None of these human relations innovations were a formal part of the CDM framework, with its focus on team problem-solving, but they were just as important in changing the atmosphere of labor-management relations and they were as much a part of encouraging worker cooperation as the teams themselves. They were thus part of a broader QWL process that went far beyond the core of CDM. As one plant manager observed, "It's getting difficult to see where [CDM] begins and ends because workers have been trained and management style has changed."

The Payoff in Productivity

For almost a year, the teams in the Transformer Department had nothing to show for their efforts. Even when one team devised a solution to a production problem, its installation met with lengthy delays. Despite this very slow transition from learning to doing, morale in the teams remained at least fair. According to a management survey, fifteen of twenty-three respondents thought that CDM "should be a permanent part of the Transformer Department," with six others indicating they were not sure. Increases in productivity in the department also suggested that the program was having some effect. In particular, the report attributed an unspecified improvement in "labor variance" (the amount of time spent actually working productively) to the presence of CDM.

Management's contention that all of these improvements derived solely from CDM needs to be viewed with caution, however. The report admits that the "new attention and involvement of management increased morale and performance," and that productivity increases may therefore have had little to do with the *direct* efforts of the CDM groups. The report concludes that management's morale-boosting influence was valuable in giving QWL "the momentum to take the innovation through its training curve until the problem-solving skills began to directly affect work changes."

Despite this, senior plant managers claimed that it was CDM itself that helped improve productivity significantly in the Transformer Department. According to one plant manager, "We went from a business that never made its schedule" to a business that was better able to fill its orders on time, mainly because management "got the hourly people understanding the *need* to service customers."

Nevertheless, the changes that the CDM groups were able to introduce formally had more to do with efficient cost controls and minor improvements in the quality of production than with any significant changes in the production process. These solutions were not expensive. As one manager noted, "The irony of the situation is that people on the shop floor are more cost-conscious than I am." Management estimated that the savings resulting from various CDM team solutions ranged from $200 to $2,000 apiece and posted these figures in the department.

Given the relatively minor significance of the production changes proposed by the CDM teams, it is interesting that the principal management exponent of QWL in the plant claimed that CDM was the main reason the Transformer Department saved $2.6 million in the second year of QWL. He could provide no backup for the conclusion, and the amount is clearly an exaggeration of the actual contributions made by the CDM teams. Presumably, this figure was meant to encourage the CDM teams and, perhaps as well, the managers who were skeptical about QWL.

Senior plant managers involved in promoting QWL also contended that it stimulated productivity gains outside the Transformer Department. For example, Universal was able to install a computerized system of inventory control "because people knew how we went about tackling problems." Salaried personnel received training and then became involved in the design of the system. The result, reported this manager, was that the plant was "the only successful case in the company of going to a computer inventory system and not getting inventories going wildly out of control."

Improved inventory control led to other cost reductions in the Transformer Department and other parts of the plant. Closer attention paid to ordering stock as it was used led to reductions in storage costs. Less time was wasted looking for stock and setting up the machines again. Other improvements associated with CDM included better welding operations and technical improvements in various jobs.

Although it is impossible to quantify accurately, there clearly have been productivity increases in the Transformer Department as well as elsewhere in the plant. Management states that the company gets more production in four days than it used to get in five. It is probably unwarranted to attribute all of this to CDM, yet, at the same time, management has certainly profited from QWL. But what about the workers?

More QWL, More Layoffs

It was not until after this first trial, which lasted eighteen months, that CDM teams were set up in two additional departments. This took place in the midst of massive layoffs. Although a senior executive reported that the layoffs had not been anticipated when CDM was initiated, they certainly should have been. The plant was obviously in serious trouble before the CDM groups were set up, and it was the threat of layoffs that helped persuade the workers to join the CDM groups in the first place. By this point, however, the layoffs hindered QWL, inhibiting its diffusion through the plant and causing a serious slump in morale.

Management chose the Switch Department as the next site for a CDM program. As in the Transformer Department, workers in Switch worked at individual benches, but here they assembled components for the switch boxes of traffic lights. The reasons for introducing CDM in Switch were similar to those in the Transformer Department: relations between workers and supervisors were less hostile than in other departments and there were fewer grievances. ("I like to head them off," the supervisor explained.) In addition, although the union remained opposed to QWL, union leaders in the department itself did not make a big issue out of it. A final attraction was that although the Switch Department was not as physically isolated as the Transformer Department, it was still small, somewhat set off from the rest of the plant, and hence relatively easy to control. As before, a failure there would have had little impact on labor-management relations elsewhere in the plant.

After choosing the Switch Department, management posted a notice explaining its intention to set up the CDM program. About forty workers (out of fifty) attended a voluntary meeting on company time. Most chose to continue with the training sessions, which took forty hours over five weeks. The revised format developed in the Transformer Department was used in the training.

Nearly half of those who began the program dropped out, some because they found the training boring or confusing, others because they did not believe that CDM would lead to meaningful changes in the quality of their working lives. Some suspected that the program was designed to benefit management at the expense of the workers. Still others dropped out because layoffs occurred even while the training was going on. Others were pushed out. One supervisor reported, "You weed out the individuals who just sit there and complain. You get somebody who can put 'em [such workers] down and you get dropouts for that reason." Skilled resource people dropped out too, some because they were not convinced that the program was important. For example, one resource person felt the potential improvements involved only "small things" and was skeptical that the CDM teams would have the power to get their solutions implemented.

By the end of the CDM training period there were only enough workers to set up two teams, one of eight members, the other of ten. Management appointed two coordinators, one of whom was a former steward in the production workers' union. This method of selection was different from that used in the Transformer Department, where any team member could volunteer to be a coordinator. In the Switch Department "we each nominated people," a supervisor remembered. "We weeded it down until there was agreement among management about [the nominee's] knowledge of handling people, which made him more capable."

Management had learned from the difficulties in the Transformer Department in other ways. The teams in the Switch Department were encouraged to focus on problems that were relatively easy to solve and that would have an immediate payoff. These specifically picked problems had obvious solutions that management could put into effect without much difficulty. For instance, one group concentrated on improving fire-safety procedures. Although management refused to install a fire-bell system because the cost was considered too great for a building that was expected to have a rather short future, progress was made in other aspects of fire safety. The other group concerned itself with improving the layout of the machines, workbenches, and stock. While not all the workers approved of the results, this second group's solutions led to easier access to stock, less congestion, and a better work flow. Housekeeping was also improved.

This generally positive beginning was not, however, enough to offset external forces that soon caused the program to founder. Continuing layoffs disrupted the teams and contributed to a growing sense of fatalism: many workers believed that there was little they could do to save their jobs, and management shared these doubts. Despite the widespread notion that increased productivity could save jobs, the more profitable operations were discontinued, while areas that had long been losing money were continued. In part this was because some of the more profitable operations were transferred to other Universal plants. In the light of this and much else, the connections between job security and productivity improvements seemed tenuous.

Eventually the coordinator of one of the groups was bumped out of the department. Members of his group were offered the chance to join the other team but decided against it, feeling that they were not likely to fit into a team that had been dealing with a different set of problems. These remaining workers became demoralized for other reasons as well, chief among them their sense that management had lost interest in their group. "We had no rules to follow" after the coordinator left, one worker reported. "We felt we were left high and dry," said another. The team soon disbanded.

Demoralization spread. Soon the remaining team was left with only three production workers, including the group leader, a worker who acted as an assistant to the supervisor. Only a few resource people stayed on. Some of the workers who dropped out complained that the team was working on problems that management should have been able to solve on its own. They also argued that some of the suggestions had been made by workers long before the teams came into being. One manager confirmed that the teams were concerned with things already "in the mill." "I haven't told them I'm working on it," he said. "A lot of my ideas come from the floor anyway." He claimed that the changes benefited team morale more than anything else, because he often made some minor improvements and "when they see it, they think that they help." He saw the improved morale as a means to a further end: "[From] the little things I can do for people that don't cost me anything, I get a lot of mileage." He estimated that there had been a 15 percent increase in production in the department but that this was mainly due to the "little things that you do for them and they're happy as hell." The CDM groups showed him "the better minds" among the workers in the department, thereby helping him to select those who could be promoted to front-line supervisory positions.

The remaining CDM team ran into further problems. While some progress was made in solving the problem of poor lighting, in other areas there were disappointing delays, partly because of the drastic decline in the number of resource people available to implement any change. In addition, the group's attempt to solve a quality-control problem led to a bitter controversy with some of the other workers. Two quality-control inspectors, neither of whom was a member of the team, were offended by a set of recommendations that the team posted in the area, which they interpreted as a direct criticism of their work. This was in part the result of the false distinction CDM made between "people problems" and "production problems": only problems that did not fall into the people-problem category were supposed to be dealt with by the CDM teams. Yet in practice it was impossible to draw neat lines between people and production. The same practical difficulty had arisen in the Transformer Department, where one of the teams had become highly critical of workers outside the department for refusing to change the way they worked in order to become part of the team's solution to a work-flow problem. The conflict was never resolved and it damaged the morale of all the workers concerned.

With only three production workers left and just two resource people coming regularly to meetings, CDM team members began to doubt that they could accomplish anything more. Management was not willing to increase the size and scope of the team, and asserted that the three remaining workers could do as much as a whole team. Management also recognized that the team was consciously avoiding any problem-solving that might lead to loss of work, and that this put serious limits on what the team could accomplish. The department supervisor was especially adamant in his opposition to the CDM teams, claiming that the workers were incapable of solving real problems and that the time they spent at CDM meetings merely created administrative headaches for him. Clearly, management was losing faith in its own creation.

One More Experiment

One further CDM group was set up in the plant, this one in part of the Wiring Department, an area where the wiring of a variety of electrical components took place. It too was unsuccessful.

As in the other departments, the labor relations climate in the Wiring Department was exceptionally good and most of the workers were receptive to CDM. However, only those in two small areas of the department were given the opportunity to join the CDM group. These were areas in which the operators had manual control over their jobs, making it possible for them to be away from their jobs without disrupting production; elsewhere in the department the jobs were mechanized and more interdependent. In addition, the automatic assembly part of the department was the plant's big producer, and management was unwilling to let the workers take time off for meetings and training sessions. Finally, the cutbacks in resource personnel in the plant were so extensive that management would have been hard pressed to find enough people to assist a larger number of workers at CDM meetings.

Initially, about fourteen production workers agreed to take part in the CDM team in the Wiring Department, yet after a month only six remained. They were soon joined by two others who had been bumped into the zone, but then several of the team's resource people dropped out. Nevertheless, the group continued to meet. It was run directly by a senior executive with expertise in worker training and labor relations. Of all the CDM groups, this was the one run most directly by management.

Eight months after the training period had ended, this team had made no tangible progress. As in the other cases, high expectations gave way to growing disillusionment, partly because no problems were being solved and partly because there were increasingly intense fears of job insecurity. Furthermore, management did not permit the teams to meet even once a week, and team members came to believe that there was little they could do to solve any problem in the department. They also wondered what they would do after they solved the one problem they were working on. (This does not mean there were no other problems. For example, bad fumes in the area were, according to union sources, the cause of numerous headaches and sore throats. The fact that this problem was not considered by the CDM team speaks volumes about the way problems were chosen.)

As in the Switch Department, the supervisor in the Wiring

Department was pleased with QWL. He saw broad spin-offs from the program, and was happy that the workers "looked for more things" to help him "get production." This was not a direct result of any problem solving by the team, however, although it was related to the aura of labor-management cooperation that the teams inspired.

Conclusion

Thus it was that a different type of QWL evolved at Universal Electric. In addition to the formal differences between the composition and decision-making processes of the CDM teams at Universal and the project committees and the booster program at Progress Motors, there were several characteristics that distinguished QWL at the two plants. Unlike the program at Progress, the QWL process at Universal was not initiated with the cooperation of the production workers' union. In contrast to the booster program at Progress, the CDM groups at Universal did not spread rapidly. Nor did they ever encompass more than a tiny fraction of the workforce: fewer than fifty of the more than four hundred production workers took part in the teams.

Finally, QWL at Universal Electric was much more experimental than at Progress. Since the future of Universal was dubious, management took advantage of the opportunity to "play" with QWL. If the experiment failed, it would die with the plant. Whether it succeeded or failed, the program would provide lessons that could be applied to the development of QWL programs in other parts of Universal's far-flung corporate empire. Indeed, this is what eventually happened: the entire plant was shut down and all the workers, including those who had been most active on the CDM teams, lost their jobs. Modified versions of CDM were subsequently applied in other Universal plants.

These were major differences. In other ways, however, the two QWL programs were similar. Both programs were initiated with the promise that the workers would benefit from better jobs and improved job security. Both were supposed to give the workers a real voice in the workplace, even though they were initiated from the top down, with most of the important decisions having been made before the workers were approached. In both cases management attempted to install projects in areas that posed the fewest risks to the overall QWL process if they should fail, and in both plants members of lower and middle management were hostile to what they saw as a threat to their authority and sometimes to their jobs.

More important from the point of view of the workers and the unions was the fact that the original QWL schemes—the CDM teams and the project committees—proved to be only a small part of the total picture. The various human relations innovations and changes in management style were part of a much larger QWL process in each plant. As we shall see in the next three chapters, these broader QWL processes not only failed to benefit most workers, but posed distinct dangers for both the workers and their unions. They were, in effect, systematic management-control strategies whose core elements were the same in both plants. It is to these overriding similarities and their effects on the workers and their unions that we now turn, for they illuminate what is fundamental about QWL: although management is beset by new technological and competitive pressures, this "new" industrial relations style is meant to solve management's age-old problem, the need to overcome workers' opposition to management controls—controls that are often as harmful to the workers as they are beneficial to their employers.

4

Empty Promises

When QWL programs were introduced at Progress Motors and Universal Electric, the core of the appeal to the workers was that they would benefit *both* management and labor—that QWL would create, in the jargon of the consultants, a "win-win" situation. At the same time that management was gaining from more and better quality production and from reduced inventory and supervisory costs, workers were supposed to be achieving better and more secure jobs and a real say in their working lives. In short, QWL promised a bloodless liberation from the tyranny of the traditional organization of work. The consultants who helped to introduce the program at Progress Motors referred to good, safe, secure jobs and democratic decision-making as "workers' rights."

These in brief were the key QWL promises. Yet, as the case histories in the previous chapters demonstrated, there were vast differences between these ideals and the reality that developed. In this chapter these differences will be examined, first in general and then in detail, in order to appreciate their implications for the workers involved, for their unions, and for organized labor as a whole.

The first big promise was that QWL would deliver the workers from jobs that were most often grindingly tedious, that gave them little or no sense of accomplishment, that presented few challenges and gave them no meaningful control over their work. Yet, except for a handful of workers at Progress Motors, there was no significant change in the way the work was organized at either plant. And because the jobs did not improve, there was no meaningful change, at either workplace, in the abysmally low levels of job satisfaction. From the point of view of those who believed the promises made by both consultants and management, QWL was a disappointing failure. Worse, at Progress Motors management dramatically increased the speed of the assembly line *after* QWL was introduced. These were cruel setbacks for workers who, because of the promises of QWL, had been led to hope for better jobs.

Unfortunately for the workers, there was even more eloquent testimony to the failure of QWL to live up to what its exponents promised. The second big promise was job security. In both plants the workers were desperate to achieve the kind of job security that would shield them from layoff at a time when double-digit unemployment was threatening to become a permanent reality. Many workers, especially at Universal Electric, were older people who knew that their chances of ever getting another job were slim. Yet instead of delivering on the promise to free them from the specter of unemployment, QWL helped to make their worst fears come true: jobs were lost in both plants, as a direct result of QWL. In the end, Universal Electric was shut down completely.

There were terrible failures, but the worst was the failure to live up to the third and greatest promise of the new industrial relations methods, the promise of industrial democracy. All other QWL promises hinged on this one because the only real protection for workers was an increase in their own power to promote their interests. Again, as in the case of job satisfaction and job security, QWL led to the opposite of what it promised. It took what little power the workers had away from them.

This was clearly the plan. There is not a single piece of evidence to support the view that QWL was directed toward meeting the promise of shared control and responsibility. The decisions that most affected workers and their unions—decisions concerning finance, product design, technological change, training and recruitment, the organization of work, research, planning, marketing strategies, and the quality and location of investments—continued to be made almost exclusively at corporate headquarters, far removed from the shop floor. Nor is there any evidence that QWL was really designed to achieve co-participation between management and workers even in decisions made at plant level. Instead, all the QWL programs focused on the restricted involvement of selected union leaders and workers in specific low-level issues that mainly concerned their motivation to achieve management's goals. Contrary to what the QWL advocates claimed, the programs were clearly designed to adjust workers to jobs, not jobs to workers. More broadly, they were designed to adjust workers to their own continuing subordination in the workplace.

The rhetoric of managers, politicians, and consultants notwithstanding, QWL involved no *power* shift in favor of union leaders or members. At the very most these programs involved the shifting of some *authority* from front-line supervisors to a few selected workers. Furthermore, just as the front-line supervisors were subordinate to the dictates of their superiors, so the few workers who were given some authority through QWL remained subordinate to higher levels of management. In addition, the major decisions about job security, working conditions, pay, and fringe benefits were still determined by a myriad of factors far beyond the influence of the workers. In neither plant did worker cooperation have any discernible impact on the company's investment decisions, since these were part of international corporate strategies determined by government policies, technological innovation, finance markets, the policies and relative strengths of competitors, the increasingly global nature of both production and demand, and a host of other variables. There was, in any event, no direct link between the firm's profits and any improvement in job security through new investments: in fact, profits were invested elsewhere and in job-displacing technology.

Even at the lowest level—the plant floor—there is no

evidence that the most basic democratic principles were respected. Majority rule, of course, was never on the agenda, but only at Progress Motors was any new form of worker representation—the project committee—introduced. However, the representatives on the project committees were never made accountable to those they represented: they were not elected on the basis of any platform; nor were they subject to election or recall. Without power of their own, they were dominated by a steering committee that was self-appointed and self-empowered. Furthermore, the preferences of the union members on the steering committee—the only people with any legitimate claim to represent the majority of workers—were subject to management veto. The only participation that either workers or union leaders were involved in was strictly consultative, involving them, at best, in minor modifications to decisions that had already been made by management. Most tellingly, the major parts of the QWL projects in both plants were installed unilaterally by management without even the pretense of consultation with labor.

Far from enhancing the ability of the workers (or the union) to influence the decisions that affected them, the whole thrust of QWL was to undermine the main form of power that workers and their unions normally resort to—the negative power of resistance or refusal to obey. QWL weakened the workers' capacity to carry on resistance activities such as work stoppages, sabotage, concerted absenteeism, and the like. This traditional power stemmed from the know-how that came with the workers' intimate understanding of their jobs, which remained despite the long history of de-skilling in both industries. This power, based on know-how, was often fortified by the solidarity that emerged from cooperation in production and from the need to resist speedups, de-skilling, unsafe working conditions, job stress, harsh supervision, and so on.

It is this capacity, as well as the workers' morale and motivation to resist, that QWL weakened in both plants. These programs encouraged a work-group identity or conformity compatible with management's goals, which in turn encouraged the development of peer pressure to counteract nonconformists (such as militants and less productive workers). Such work-group identity also kept work groups apart, so that solidarity had less chance to broaden across the plant and workers remained isolated in groups that were more easily controlled.

In addition, QWL undermined the chance for any increase in worker power by fostering a weakened steward structure. As front-line supervisors were encouraged to make informal deals with workers, the stewards' grievance-handling functions withered. This also undermined the stewards' mediating role between front-line supervisors and workers. At Universal Electric, management co-opted some stewards into CDM teams; a few even became team coordinators. Finally, on top of the Jekyll-and-Hyde role that stewards had to play, as both adversaries of management and as QWL mediators, in both plants they were called on to deal with QWL-inspired demands to discipline workers who did not conform.

Further weakening the power of workers and their unions was the tendency of QWL to turn collective interests into a multitude of separate and sometimes conflicting demands. The quality-booster program at Progress Motors was the prime example of this: much of what the boosters gained, the repair workers and others lost, while the boosters became a separate and privileged layer of the workforce. In addition, there was a tendency for work groups to compete with each other; accommodations made by supervisors in one area helped to incite envy between work groups and zones. The scramble for job security, which already divided workers on the basis of seniority, only reinforced such divisions.

Finally, QWL led to a weakening of unity in the union leadership, particularly at Progress Motors. Because neither the leaders nor the members were given a clear understanding of QWL, and because QWL was from first to last a top-down affair, a major backlash occurred and it was directed primarily against the union leaders. Even after a large and bitter majority of the membership decided to pull out, the divisions that had been created within the leadership endured and workers lost confidence in some of the best and most experienced leaders they had. Meanwhile, QWL programs continued without the union. At Universal Electric, QWL also led to a weakening of unity in the union leadership, although to a less serious degree. The whole tendency of QWL is to undermine genuine unions, altering their adversarial style and their collective bargaining and grievance functions—and in the process threatening their future.

Such, in general, were the contrasts between QWL's promises and its reality. These contrasts bear a closer look, however, if we are to understand the various ways in which these "workers' rights" were translated into worse jobs, lost jobs, disappointed hopes, misplaced trust, conflicts between workers, divisions within the union leadership, a passive acceptance of technological change, and an increasing confusion about the fundamental reasons for trade unionism and the direction the labor movement should take.

The Impact on Job Satisfaction

First, Progress Motors. As we saw earlier, very few workers at the plant felt that QWL had improved their jobs and increased their sense of work satisfaction. The most emphatically positive reactions were voiced by some of the project committee members in Trim and by some of the quality boosters. A few said that as a result of QWL they had actually come to look forward to going to work—a startling revelation in a workplace where assembly-line jobs were so clearly bad. (The "enjoyment, accomplishment, and pride," the "optimal variety," the "challenge and ongoing opportunities to learn" that the consultants offered still had to be squeezed into a job that was repeated every 1.3 minutes.) A few workers also reported that their involvement in QWL had led to dramatic improvements in their self-confidence, and credited it to the greater opportunity the program gave them to use their talents at work. In addition, some of the problem-solving techniques that were taught to project committee members proved useful outside the plant, and this helped make non-work life a bit more satisfying.

At the other end of the spectrum were the reactions of some members of the project committees in Paint, who felt that QWL had led to a decline in job satisfaction. "We felt we'd been in this a year and got nothing," one project committee member said. "We'd gone to these meetings and interrupted our private time at home and got nothing. I'd rather stay at home. We figure we were cheated." He felt that there had been no improvement in the pace or the quality of work: "Why should you change for the company when the company isn't giving you anything?" Another project committee member reported that the committee members were "made to look like assholes to the guys on the line. We got nothing out of it," he complained. "Not only did the company let us down, but we in turn let the guys down and got criticized for leading them down the garden path."

Yet only in a minority of cases did QWL lead to discernible increases or decreases in job satisfaction. The great majority of the workers involved in the pilot projects experienced no meaningful change in job satisfaction whatsoever. It is not difficult to account for this. In most instances there was no significant change in the jobs themselves, and what few improvements there were concerned marginal, mainly cosmetic, aspects of work life. For example, workers in the Trim Zone at Progress Motors generally regarded the music speakers as an improvement over the radios they had brought to work. They also appreciated cleaner work areas, cleaner and better ventilated washrooms, and newly painted posts and ceilings, but these were environmental changes that were not directly related to the job. A few also mentioned that they appreciated better tools, work clothes, and more convenient job layouts. Occasionally they had a chance to improve the quality of their work, but the most significant job change for most workers in Trim was temporary: it occurred when workers learned new jobs in the first phase of job rotation.

None of this came close to the on-the-job improvements that

the workers had expected. Furthermore, what few satisfactions QWL did deliver were tempered by the workers' sense that it was in management's interest to make such changes. In other words, most workers saw the program as a smokescreen for implementing management's own goals. For instance, most of the workers did not believe that the opportunity to improve product quality was due to QWL. Instead, they saw this as the direct result of the priority management had earlier decided to place on quality over quantity—a change dictated by growing consumer dissatisfaction with the poor quality of the company's cars. They also felt that other changes that were credited to QWL should have been implemented through the health-and-safety committee, which the union was already operating jointly with management. The QWL program was therefore unnecessary.

At the same time, there was a recognition that, without management's support for QWL, such improvements as there were would probably not have been made. Thus one worker spoke of better tool maintenance in his area as "piddle shit, because the union should have been able to get this without a QWL committee," but he went on to point out that such "garbage issues," which had never been brought to the union before, were brought to the project committees. Management made these small concessions in order to give the workers the sense that their suggestions were not being made in vain.

Reports of improved job satisfaction frequently turned out to be totally unrelated to any changes in job content. For example, the workers on the A shift in Trim felt somewhat more satisfied with their jobs as a result of QWL than did the workers on the B shift. The main reason for this was that the supervisor on the A shift was friendlier, more competent, and more trustworthy than a series of supervisors on the other shift. Similarly, the workers who helped to set up the pilot project in Trim tended to feel greater satisfaction than the workers who inherited it. The more positive attitude of the veterans arose because they regarded themselves as the founding fathers of the project. Seniority was another factor affecting perceptions. Workers with more seniority tended to have better jobs and to be better adjusted to them. They therefore saw less benefit in such changes as job rotation than did workers with less-preferred jobs. Those who learned job rotation generally felt that it was not worth implementing: as one worker put it, "I'd rather do one shitty job than three shitty jobs!" Taking external factors such as these into account, genuine improvements in actual job satisfaction were hard to come by.

There was one exception: the quality boosters were without doubt beneficiaries of QWL because their jobs clearly did improve. Yet even here there was a steep falling-off in job satisfaction over time. One booster wondered if "everything is just a pipe dream or pie-in-the-sky." Another grumbled that management had promised him that he would not be used to fill in for workers who needed first aid or wanted to talk to their steward, yet his supervisor made him do the jobs of absent workers every day. "The supervisors violate [the agreement] to cover their asses, so no [cars needing] repairs go out of the zone," he complained. "So we're not getting the full results of the program that *we* should get." Most tellingly, much of the "job enrichment" that was added to the boosters' jobs was at the expense of the repair workers or front-line supervisors, so even the quality-booster program could not be considered an *overall* improvement in jobs.

Those involved in the project committees and those who became quality boosters comprised a tiny fraction of the total workforce. For the vast majority of workers, QWL meant no positive change at all. Even as you read this, the assembly line continues, the jobs are still restricted to mind-numbing, repetitive movements, and the pace is more than one-third faster than it was before the QWL program was installed. By almost any objective measure, job satisfaction at Progress Motors remains the lowest of almost any company in the industry, QWL or no QWL.

Now consider the impact of QWL on jobs at Universal Electric. The consultant who set up the original CDM program promised that it would lead to an improved quality of work life and a demonstrable increase in job satisfaction. Indeed, he promised that jobs would improve to the point where the workers would find them interesting and meaningful.

As at Progress Motors, there were a few workers who greeted QWL with considerable enthusiasm, especially at first. One of these workers wrote a letter explaining his feelings:

> Ever since I was fourteen years old, I have worked in a factory or shop in one business or another, except for a few years I served as a soldier in Canada's armed services.
>
> I have always done what I was told to do, even though I was most often a little resentful of being told. The last few years I have found that most supervisors now *ask me* to do something, and if I know how to do the job I am allowed to do as I see fit, as long as I do the job properly.
>
> With Cooperative Decision-Making I think that Canadian industry can use the brain power of all the people involved. . . . As employees of the company *we* will be able to input into most of the planning of what is to be done at our place of employment. We will not only do the job but we will know why we do the job, and just where we fit in the whole system. *That is why I participate.*

Management told the workers that QWL would allow them to use their brain power on the job and would give them greater autonomy. In practice, however, about the only positive part of QWL was its human relations aspect—its more humane, less authoritarian supervisory style. "They listen now," one member of a CDM team explained. "They don't think we're a bunch of dummies on the floor here." But this had far less to do with the content of the decisions being made than with the style in which they were enforced. Management style was less "autocratic" than before and more "catalytic," so workers were less often "a little resentful of being told" (to quote the worker's letter).

The workers who felt that QWL was beneficial generally agreed that this was because of the cosmetic changes in the work environment. They pointed to cleaner work areas, better lighting, and a better "attitude" in the workplace. It is clear that this marginal improvement in job satisfaction for these few did not result from better jobs because, despite management's claim that at Universal Electric "nobody's job is the same," no job changed that much. So the promise that QWL would deliver better jobs was an empty one. Those who appreciated the cosmetic changes were almost always CDM team members, even though the changes affected everyone in the department. This suggests that the positive feelings that these few workers had about QWL were due to something other than the environmental changes themselves—perhaps to the attention they received from management.

None of this is new. For decades sophisticated managers have reverted to coercion only as a last resort. Furthermore, it has long been widely held that simple attention from management tends to motivate workers to increase production. Managers and industrial sociologists even have a name for this phenomenon: it is called the "Hawthorne effect," after research done at the Hawthorne Works of Western Electric in Illinois during the 1920s and 1930s. Analysts of these experiments concluded that special attention from management and the research team had, in effect, flattered workers into increasing their output. This had absolutely nothing to do with improvements in the workers' jobs and everything to do with management's exercise of power in more subtle, more effective ways. Such manipulation is old hat. It does not require a new name.

The Impact on Job Security

The consultants at Progress and Universal also promised that QWL would deliver improved job security. It was this promise above all that attracted workers in both plants to the program. Many at Progress Motors had just returned from a year-long

layoff and knew that massive layoffs were continuing throughout the industry. Similarly, major layoffs had been taking place
at Universal Electric for years, and the workforce there had
already been reduced to a fraction of its former size. The rest of
the workers generally were in their fifties and sixties and knew
that they had next to no chance of finding other jobs. Consequently, workers in both plants were very receptive to this
particular promise.

The workers were told that their salvation lay in beating their
firms' foreign competitors. If they cooperated with management—through QWL—their plants would be more productive,
sales would improve, profits would increase, there would be new
investments and therefore more jobs—and the great fear of
unemployment would ease.

The first hint of a discrepancy between this new "workers'
right" and reality at Progress Motors came almost at the beginning, when management refused to provide a legally binding
guarantee that the program would not eliminate jobs. This
ominous sign proved to be prophetic when the QWL program
directly contributed to the loss of four jobs from an area next to
the project in Trim. A senior manager estimated that, since the
beginning of the project, repairs to products leaving the project
area had been reduced by about 50 percent, a reduction he
considered "absolutely out of this world." He explained that
although there were some additional factors contributing to the
elimination of these jobs, QWL was the main cause: "We wouldn't
have been able to do it if the defect rate hadn't gone down."
Other jobs were lost throughout the plant because workers were
more inclined to cooperate with the introduction of labor-saving
technology.

The situation at Universal Electric was even worse: the whole
plant was shut down. QWL did not save a single job.

No doubt major job losses will continue to take place in both
companies, as well as throughout the automotive and electrical
industries. This will occur *regardless* of QWL. Whereas, at best,
QWL can influence only small-scale short-term gains in productivity, job security depends upon long-term and fundamen-

tal political and economic forces: the changing relations between competitors on a world scale, shifting patterns of
international trade, the development of new technologies, the
stability of international financial institutions, and a host of
other factors that workers are in no position to influence. It will
be managers, not workers, who decide on the appropriate policies for Progress and Universal to follow, and they will do so
primarily in the light of what they believe to be their own
interests and those of their shareholders. When choices are
made between buying robots or hiring workers, between importing
parts and services from nonunion sources or providing them "in
house," between new investment in the companies' old plants or
shifting capital out to more profitable ventures, QWL will figure
as only one small part (if it figures at all) in management's most
important decisions.

The Impact on Worker Solidarity and the Union

The third promise was that of "participation" or "the right to
have some say over all things that affect you." This was the
heart of the QWL ideal, an ideal of—in the words of the
consultants at Progress Motors—"democratic principles in the
workplace . . . based on joint control and shared responsibility
between union and management at all levels."

There is only one way in which QWL could have helped the
workers to achieve democracy in their workplaces: by helping
them to achieve greater power. This would have required greater unity among the workers and, at the same time, a greater
awareness of where their collective interests lay—in short,
greater solidarity. In practice, QWL accomplished the opposite.
It systematically weakened worker power in both plants by
fostering, and at the same time obscuring, a shift toward greater
management control.

Progress Motors

In assessing the impact of QWL on the workers' relations with each other, it is important to understand that *worker solidarity* cannot always be equated with *work-group cohesion*. As will be seen, it is possible for an increase in the cohesion of a work group to constitute a *decline* in solidarity if that work group is in conflict with other work groups or with the interests of workers in the plant or in the union as a whole. This would be the case if work-group cohesion were attached to the promotion of management goals that were contrary to the workers' collective interests. If increasing cohesion were to be built, for instance, around a dedication to accelerated speedups, compulsory overtime, the replacement of jobs by machines, the waiving of occupational health and safety protections, and so on, all in the name of cooperation with management, and if workers received little or nothing in return, this would normally be considered antithetical to worker solidarity.

Some of the increase in cohesion among workers in Trim represented a (less dramatic) case in point. While some of the workers there—especially older, more established workers who did not speak English very well—felt that QWL had no impact on their relations with other workers, most workers reported that they had become a more closely knit group. In particular, they felt that the orientation meetings gave them a valuable opportunity to get to know one another better and that the regular discussions and decision-making led them into more meaningful communication with each other. In addition, some felt that tension between militants and nonmilitants was reduced because cooperation with the supervisor became more legitimate for everyone. As one worker observed, "After QWL, nobody laughs at good workers." It was reported that this was accomplished by a greater sense of involvement in the pursuit of goals such as improved product quality, and that it resulted in more mutual aid among workers.

Workers in Trim also pointed to a reduction in what they

called "shift-itis": various conflicts between workers on opposite shifts, usually between those who did the same jobs. For instance, one worker would "build ahead" so that by the shift's end he would have a surplus. It was not uncommon for him to return the next day to find that his counterpart on the other shift had used up the surplus without replacing it. Other conflicts concerned the hoarding or misuse of tools. The advent of QWL sometimes reduced this kind of shift-itis because the workers had a chance to get to know each other at orientation sessions. In order to foster further reductions in tension, the project committees made a point of working together so that decisions made on behalf of one shift would be agreeable to workers on the other.

The reduction in these conflicts was consistent with management's goal of increased productivity, and quite a few of these workers began to see themselves as members of the Progress Motors "family." The greater cohesiveness in the zone was not, therefore, part of an increase in worker solidarity in the sense described above. The workers in Trim did not yet know that their pursuit of greater productivity had already led to a loss of four jobs in a nearby area, but it is likely that, had the project continued, more of the latent conflicts between the goals of QWL and the workers' interests would have emerged.

Indeed, some of those conflicts had already emerged as a countervailing influence that undermined cohesion in Trim. In particular, QWL caused an increase in friction between workers with different amounts of seniority. Probably because of their greater experience, some of those with higher seniority were more suspicious of management's motives and less wholehearted in their cooperation with QWL. Since those with more seniority often had the better jobs, they were more anxious that job rotation and a QWL-inspired redistribution of work loads would endanger their jobs. Opposing them were those with less seniority and with relatively worse jobs who tended to regard these changes more favorably.

Another source of friction among Trim workers was the intensified production rivalry between the shifts. Supervisors

on opposite shifts had been promoting this kind of competition
long before the QWL project was set up, but QWL made it more
appealing, at least to some workers. As a result, those who
regarded it as a voluntary speedup were critical of those of their
fellow workers who were caught up in it.

Solidarity in both Paint and Trim was also weakened by
increasing tensions between committee members and some of
their constituents. Many workers envied the committee members' privileges and the attention they received from management. Some also criticized the project committees on the ground
that individual committee members were unqualified for their
positions. Although project committee meetings were supposed
to be open to all, some workers complained that their committee
representatives were being favored with time off or overtime
pay for meetings that did not produce enough benefits. These
criticisms intensified when project committee members went on
trips and to training seminars. Not a few workers felt that the
committees had too intimate a relationship with senior managers. The more the projects floundered, the more this type of
dissatisfaction grew.

The friction between the workers and their representatives
on the project committees also derived from a conflict of interest
that at first seemed unimportant. Committee members benefited from holding their meetings during work hours so that those
in car pools would not be inconvenienced, but this created
difficulties for those workers who remained on the job. To fill in
for the committee members, some workers had to accept temporary reassignment to jobs they did not like. Some also complained that it was more difficult to get emergency help.

On top of this, there was another built-in source of friction:
because each project committee was supposed to represent the
majority, minority interests were sometimes sacrificed. This
happened, for example, when priorities were set from among the
suggestions workers made for improvements. Another source of
strain lay in the sense of superior status that management
encouraged in some project committee members. For instance,
sometimes management personnel would ask committee mem-

bers to keep information from their fellow workers. Such confidences helped to breed a "them and us" attitude on the part of committee members toward their own constituents.

The most significant dimension of the decline in solidarity, however, was between those zones with pilot projects and those without. Workers in Trim in particular reported a new tension in their relationship with the skilled maintenance workers who serviced their machines and tools. They believed that the maintenance workers saw QWL as a potential threat to their jobs. If cooperation on behalf of product quality were to spill over into a situation where zealous production workers repaired and maintained their own machines, the skilled workers' jobs might well have been jeopardized. This was of particular concern to the skilled-trades workers because they recognized that the production workers often knew a great deal about the maintenance and repair of their tools. If this knowledge were put at management's disposal, the jealously guarded boundaries between skilled and less-skilled workers would be seriously eroded. Skilled maintenance workers were especially sensitive about this because new technologies had already rendered some of their skills obsolete.

Workers in Trim also sensed a deterioration in their relations with nearby production workers. "Most guys think we're a bunch of assholes," a worker from Trim acknowledged, agreeing with another who said they were considered to be "suckholes." Early on, Trim had been dubbed the "Flower Zone," partly on account of its brightly painted posts and girders, but more pointedly because workers outside the zone likened worker-management cooperation to a "hippie love-in." Workers in Trim blamed this attitude on their neighbors' jealousy and ignorance of what was really going on, but they resented the fact that all the publicity surrounding the program gave them the feeling of "living in a fishbowl."

Despite all this, the impact of the pilot projects on worker solidarity was negligible compared to the impact of the quality-booster program. In retrospect, it is clear that this program was the core of management's real (and largely hidden) QWL agenda.

Unlike the pilot projects, which provided little in the way of real change in the jobs themselves, the boosters' jobs were qualitatively improved. This improvement was much more than that offered by job rotation because it incorporated some responsibility for low-level planning and for the organization of work among the eight or ten workers within each booster's jurisdiction. It thereby provided a narrow bridge into what had previously been the sole preserve of the front-line supervisors.

This meant that there was an intrinsic conflict between the quality booster as worker and the quality booster as supervisor. One booster explained that he had trained a certain worker to do a job but that he was not doing it properly at the end of the training period. Although he was convinced that the worker was behaving this way on purpose, the booster was unwilling to report the problem to his supervisor. His only alternative was to continue helping the worker by repairing the work himself, even though this put a heavy burden on him.

This tension was inherent. Since the booster was charged with resolving problems that interfered with the quality of work in his area, it was his responsibility to report problems that he could not solve to his supervisor. When another worker was responsible for the problem, the booster could choose between adding to his own work or offending members of his group. There were thus very narrow limits set on how far a successful booster could go in either direction. A booster who helped his fellow workers too often was a "sucker," while a booster who took a delinquent worker to the supervisor was a "fink." A booster who did neither was not a booster.

This contradiction between being a worker and acting like a supervisor led to a great deal of conflict within the work groups. Even in the program's early stages, workers were referring to boosters as "supervisors without ties," and some workers were sarcastic about quality boosters who were coming to work "dressed up like the high-paid help"—i.e., management. A manager, on the other hand, called them "a union within a union." Conflicts soon came out into the open. Union leaders, many of whom had previously supported QWL, reported a sharp increase in "finking" as a result of the booster program. Fistfights between workers also erupted, something that had been exceedingly rare before the booster program was introduced. (Fighting on the job generally led to dismissal or a long suspension.)

Under these circumstances, management's power was bound to increase. Where disputes within work groups undermined solidarity, management control increased. And where a more cohesive work group cooperated with the boosters, management's control objectives were also served. Furthermore, irrespective of whether QWL initiatives like these brought about cohesive work groups or fighting and increased bickering and tension, there was little chance that traditional solidarity could be forged *between* work groups. As long as the work groups were isolated and inward looking, there could be no serious movement toward solidarity across the plant. From management's point of view this was absolutely crucial, since it was only on the basis of linkages between zones and departments, and solidarity across the plant, that workers could pose a threat to overall management control. Far more than the pilot projects, the booster program helped to deliver management from this fear.

The QWL program also presented management with major opportunities to undermine the union leadership and even the union itself. From the beginning, QWL at Progress Motors contained several implicit dangers for the union. These dangers were partly "political," in the sense that they affected the electoral fortunes of individual union leaders and leadership factions, but at a deeper level they concerned the very structure of union representation and the future of collective bargaining.

The pilot projects contained the first such dangers, but to those union leaders on the steering committee they seemed minimal. After all, they had the formal right to veto any projects. Besides, although the project committees supposedly represented workers in the zones, they were in practice subordinate to the steering committee, where the union had an equal voice with management.

Nevertheless, such formal controls did not in themselves eliminate the project committees' threat to the union, especially since the committees could become a partial substitute for the union's grievance procedure. As bodies that elicited the workers' views and concerns, the project committees were a way for the workers to express their needs on an ongoing basis. The articulation of workers' needs is one of the main functions of collective bargaining, but collective bargaining at Progress Motors, as elsewhere, has always been sporadic, with intervals of two and three years between sessions. Furthermore, most workers had, at best, only an arms-length relationship to the collective bargaining process. Bargaining was done for them, not by them, and it was done by leaders and staff they rarely knew. For these reasons, there was always the danger that the pilot projects would lead to the informal takeover of crucial parts of collective bargaining.

The danger did not come to pass, mainly because the pilot projects never spread beyond two zones. In addition, the crucial weakness of the project committees lay less in their relation to the steering committee than in the fragility of their ties to the workers they were supposed to represent. The project committees had no clear mandate from their constituents and, aside from informal contact, the only consultation the workers had with the committees occurred every few months when management held a workshop for the workers and project committees in the plant cafeteria or at a hotel. It was only on these rare occasions that most workers were asked to talk about what was "bugging" them.

The structural weaknesses in the project committees made it difficult for management to take advantage of the dangers these committees held for the union. In order to do that, management would have had to give rank-and-file workers far more authority on the committees. It is an important irony that the whole top-down nature of this supposed experiment in economic democracy prevented this.

As it was, the committees were management's dependent, and could accomplish nothing without management's support. Informally, management's control of the project committees went further, even to the point where management's own agenda was adopted by the committees. This was done "in a small, subtle way," one manager confided, "getting it to be their [the representatives'] idea." But here again management's attempt to increase control was self-limiting: Progress Motors would have had to give the project committees far more autonomy if they were to serve as a more formidable extension of management control. Instead, management's influence was so obviously great that it took away much of the legitimacy that the committees might otherwise have had in the workers' eyes. It was thus virtually impossible for the committees to gain the degree of popular confidence they would have needed to replace the union leaders, especially the stewards.

This is not to say that these flaws in management's design could not have been corrected. It is not at all difficult to imagine the kind of threat a widely diffused system of project committees could have posed to the union if management had given the committees the authority to resolve on-the-job problems. The spread of such committees across the plant could easily have become the basis of a collaborationist company-style union.

The danger to the union leadership at Progress Motors was also reduced by the stewards' finesse in walking the tightrope between their more adversarial role as union representatives and their more cooperative role as members of the project committees. They were able to do this in part because their role on the committees was peripheral. As one worker who served on a project committee observed, "The steward wasn't really supposed to be involved except to sit in and make sure that there was no crossing over into union territory." In other words, the stewards retained the main role of guarding the collective bargaining agreement. Moreover, because the various QWL meetings provided them with many opportunities to get to know their constituents better, the stewards generally strengthened their ties to the workers in the project zones.

On the other hand, the stewards, particularly in Trim, had to be very careful that QWL did not cause their relations with constituents *outside* the zone to deteriorate. Each steward typically represented over two hundred workers in five or six zones. Outside the zone, the stewards were open to the same criticisms as the workers in the projects. One union leader reported that he had to be very careful that news about various "deals" worked out in the project committee did not leak out. While these deals may not have violated the contract, they did provide benefits exclusively for the workers in only one zone. If these arrangements had become known to workers outside the zone, and to the stewards' political rivals, they would almost certainly have become the basis of a major political division within the local union leadership.

Furthermore, if the QWL projects had spread across the plant, the stewards would have been placed in a losing situation on several fronts at the same time. Either the project committees would have operated relatively autonomously from the stewards, in effect substituting for them, or the stewards would have been absorbed by the committees, in which case their time and energies would have been taken away from their union responsibilities. Like the boosters, who were at once workers and bosses, stewards who continued to play both their adversarial and their cooperative roles would sooner or later have had to face a fundamental identity problem. Were they union stewards or QWL coordinators?

In the end, QWL did become a major source of division within the local leadership. Increasingly bitter attacks were leveled at those leaders who served on the steering committee for "selling out" the membership. Other attacks were directed at the stewards in Trim and Paint who cooperated with the project committees, and at local leaders who had taken advantage of the various opportunities associated with QWL, such as visiting other plants and attending weekend retreats in hotels where QWL seminars were given. The anti-QWL faction quickly grew from a vociferous minority to a righteous majority of the local leadership. There was increasing opposition from among the general membership as well, many of whom knew very little about the QWL program until then. Eventually a majority of the union leadership decided to "put QWL on the back burner," and then to pull out of the project entirely.

Although this too led to criticism of the union leadership, especially from pro-QWL elements in Trim, the negative impact of the decision was not great. While a management poll showed that 96 percent of the workers in Trim wanted to continue the project, this desire was accompanied by a call for major reforms, including the replacement of the project committees by voluntary and more informal bodies. Furthermore, Trim was the only area in the plant where there was much support for the project. Indeed, the decision to pull out of the pilot projects was very popular there as well as across the rest of the plant, except among the boosters.

Even though the union pulled out of the projects in Trim and Paint, QWL in its most well developed form—the booster program—continued. The dangers that the booster program held for the union leadership were far, far greater than those posed by the pilot projects. The program had strong company backing, and was firmly in place throughout the plant. Because it was introduced unilaterally by the company, the union leadership had no say about how it was developed. Union leaders who had entered into the QWL game hoping to win discovered that the game was not quite what it seemed. Management began the quality-booster program as a new offensive, scoring first with an end run around the union.

The main threat to the union was that the boosters would become what one manager had said they were, "a union within a union." Since the boosters had considerable seniority and long experience in the plant, and since they also had qualities that made them "natural leaders," they were the sort of people who might otherwise have found themselves in elected union positions. The boosters generally had a much closer relationship to the eight or ten workers they worked with than did the stewards, who serviced over two hundred workers and therefore were able to have only occasional and limited connection to those they represented. The boosters, on the other hand, were in constant contact with their groups throughout the working day. In addition, the boosters' dealings with their fellow workers were not restricted to problems directly relevant to the collective bargaining agreement.

More important for the union was the tendency for the line between workers and bosses to become blurred as the cooperative efforts of the booster program habituated workers to images of a new sense of industrial harmony. This blurring masked enduring conflicts of interest, giving a one-big-happy-family face to the exercise of management power. Meanwhile, the actual power relationship and the distribution of the benefits of production between the workers, on the one hand, and the managers and shareholders on the other, remained the same.

Union leaders tried to persuade management to eliminate the booster program but were disregarded. The program remains to this day, and continues to present the most serious danger to the union. If this program and the exaggerated sense of harmony it promotes should prevail, it will foster the kind of false peace in the workplace that has typically bred weak unionism—or no unionism at all. It is no accident that the vast majority of QWL programs are in workplaces without unions.

Whether these threats materialize will depend on how the inherently contradictory relationship between the boosters and the workers is resolved. It is quite possible that the booster program will move in the same direction as the QWL programs that have existed in nonunion plants in the United States since the 1950s—programs now found in many unionized auto plants. Selected workers and union leaders in these plants, called "quality operators," help management select their supervisors (who are called "team coordinators"). The workers also directly elect assistant supervisors from among their own ranks. If this is the direction the booster program takes, then "team consciousness" will indeed camouflage the differences between "us" and "them." To the extent that the Progress Motors booster becomes a successful practitioner of the human relations approach and the workers come to see themselves as allied with management, the threat to the union's legitimacy with the workers will be very great. The boosters themselves may well become the skeleton around which an informal pro-management "union" forms, or they may become part of a movement to take over the local union from within, or, in the worst-case scenario, they may become the spearhead of a union decertification campaign.

Even before QWL, the union at Progress Motors—the United Auto Workers—was vulnerable. The connection between union leadership and membership has been weak for many years, especially in the United States. Although this is less true of the UAW than it is of many other unions, and less true of this particular local than of other locals, even here only a declining minority of members, almost all on the verge of retirement, have any memory of the struggle to establish the local, much less the union as a whole. The majority had to join the union as a condition of employment. Most never attended general membership meetings unless there was a strike or a proposed increase in the compulsory dues checkoff. Their main link to the union was through the steward, and that connection was, as we have seen, often fragile. The steward's chief function is to use his or her knowledge and expertise about the rules in the contract to help settle conflicts, either informally or through the grievance procedure, and most workers, most of the time, are not involved in such conflicts. Furthermore, the grievance rate is now at an all-time low in the local, and QWL will certainly not lead to its rise.

Where QWL programs are successful, the workers will clearly feel less and less need for a union to police the provisions of the collective bargaining agreement. With management and workers allied in the push to increase productivity—the one on behalf of profits, the other on behalf of a dubious pursuit of job security—a loss of respect for the contract's provisions is inevitable. And if workers believe that provisions for health and safety, rest periods, time standards, and the like interfere with the overall goal of reducing the costs of production, they will find themselves making even greater concessions on the job than their union makes at the bargaining table. For similar reasons, they are likely to be less willing to demonstrate solidarity with fellow workers who, because of alcohol or drug addiction, or psychological or physical problems, act as a drag on productivity. All of this continues to be a clear threat to the union, to the workers, and to the leadership.

QWL also continues to threaten the union because it breeds a host of informal accommodations between workers and supervisors. To some extent, such accommodation took place before the advent of QWL. For example, even before the program was introduced, some workers were allowed to leave work early if they produced more than the average. If management requested it, some traded their relief breaks and holidays for overtime pay. In other cases, supervisors overlooked lateness. Such "deals" between workers and supervisors contributed to an unevenness in labor-management relations that fostered envy, especially where favoritism was involved, and reinforced differences among workers based on age, ethnicity, seniority, and other factors. They also made it much more difficult for the union to enforce a uniform set of contract rules and lessened the ability of the leaders to appeal to common problems and perceptions among the members.

This is likely to be only the beginning. Over time, QWL will lead to the spread of such informal accommodations and their adverse effects will become more pronounced. There is a host of petty supervisory practices and work arrangements that the workers dislike but that cannot be effectively resolved through grievance procedures, either because they are part of "management's rights" to manage or because the grievance procedure is too delay-ridden, uncertain, and biased in favor of management. They can be at least partly resolved through QWL—but by management alone, and outside the contract. These problems are often specific to an area or to an individual. They may involve details about the way a job is set up or a preference for a particular kind of tool or piece of work clothing. While there is some room in the collective bargaining agreement for local issues, these needs are far too numerous and petty for this level of bargaining, which is in any case too intermittent and removed from the shop floor to be useful. It is here, right at this Achilles heel of organized labor, that QWL threatens the union.

The multiplication of such arrangements presents another fundamental danger to the union. To the extent that management delivers improvements on this informal basis while at the same time forcing concessions at the bargaining table, the union will appear obsolete. Rather than seeing QWL as a gain made by the union through collective bargaining (a view the union may at first be anxious to promote, as a trade-off for contract concessions), the workers are likely to regard it as a partial or even total substitute for collective bargaining itself.

QWL provides still other openings for undermining the unity of the local leadership, and for weakening the links between the local and higher levels. The main difficulties stem from the union's lack of control over the way in which QWL develops, a clear reflection of the union's inferior power in relation to management. As we have seen, QWL was not initiated with the educated understanding or participation of the majority of the union—leadership or membership. Some of the most influential and able local leaders (referred to as "key players" by the QWL consultants) constituted the core of the union's backing for the pilot projects, but the rest of the leadership only assented (more or less passively) and did not participate in developing or carrying the program forward. From the outset this support was shallow and thus subject to sudden reversal. Consequently, the unity of both the leadership and the membership was highly vulnerable.

The growing threat to the union meant that the leadership's support for QWL could not be taken for granted. Both consultants and management realized this, but too late to do much to correct it. Once it was recognized, the consultants hosted a two-

and-a-half-day workshop at an expensive hotel where small group sessions were set up to deal with the union leaders' fears and concerns. At least some union people came away less suspicious of QWL, but there was no follow-up. "That's when people [dissident local union leaders] started throwing the hatchets," one leader observed.

Because the union members of the steering committee took part in a process they could not control, and because they did so without strong support from either their membership or the other union leaders, they were open to attack from their own side. When management did not deliver the expected improvements and did not diffuse the pilot projects beyond the two zones, these leaders became the target of growing criticism—criticism that was never adequately refuted. Eventually a strong majority of the union leadership rejected further participation in the pilot projects, leaving the supporters of QWL compromised, both personally and politically.

QWL also undermined union unity because it prompted a scramble for the various management gifts associated with it: trips abroad to investigate other QWL projects, all-expenses-paid conferences in luxury hotels, time off without loss of pay to take training courses. One senior union leader even went with the plant manager on a fact-finding tour of Japan. Competition for such perquisites quickly generated discord within the leadership—and not a few workers saw them as a way of "buying off" their representatives.

Finally, QWL posed another threat that had, and still has, the most profound implications for the union. QWL claimed to provide protection from job loss, the main issue facing the union and the concern that had the very highest priority among the workers. The notion that greater cooperation on behalf of greater productivity would ensure their jobs had an aura of common sense that enticed and goaded many workers. If union leaders accepted this promise and supported QWL—and yet jobs were nevertheless lost—they would be held to account. If the union leaders did not support QWL and jobs were lost, the result would be the same. Since there is no doubt that jobs will continue to be lost in many of the company's plants—QWL or no—the union leadership is locked into a no-win situation. This double bind continues to bedevil not only the union leaders at this plant but their counterparts throughout the industry.

There are a great many other locals in the UAW that take part in similar QWL programs. The problem that both the union leadership and the membership must face in this ongoing quest for job security through increased cooperation with management is that the spread of QWL throughout other plants pits workers in one against workers in others, all of them caught up in a desperate bid to save jobs and to keep ahead of the layoff treadmill that has been oiled by QWL. Such competition has already led to local bargaining over productivity issues and undermined industrywide collective bargaining agreements as locals line up against each other in bidding wars to see which ones can offer their employers the most concessions. In effect, workers in different plants have been played off against each other to achieve greater profits. The result has been massive disunity within the union, especially above the local level.

QWL has already contributed to disunity within the international United Automobile Workers union as a whole. The UAW's executive board divided over QWL, as well as other issues, when Donald Ephlin, the former head of the union's Ford section, tried to succeed Douglas Fraser as UAW president. Ephlin's enthusiastic support for QWL gave him a reputation for being a "captive of management," which contributed to his failure to gain the presidency. QWL has also contributed to the breakup of the UAW as an international union. At the time of research, the workers at the Progress Motors plant were members of the UAW but in 1985 their local (along with other Canadian UAW locals) broke away to form an independent national union, the Canadian Auto Workers (CAW). The Canadians did so largely because they felt that the U.S. leadership was heading in a direction that was too closely allied with management—and that QWL programs, which were (and are) far more prevalent in the U.S. auto industry than in Canada, were at the core of the

U.S. UAW's quest to help restore U.S. competitiveness through concessions bargaining and greater labor-management cooperation.

It seems likely that the ties binding other sections of the union will also loosen and that locals will go their own way, either to defend themselves from such pressures through greater militancy or to compete with each other by setting up what will be, in essence, company unions. If workers see their interests primarily in local terms, and if there is no overall union strategy to prevent the locals from competing with each other for jobs, the UAW, once the highly centralized standard-bearer of the labor movement, will become a federation of warring locals. Such a union cannot long survive.

For all of these reasons, QWL at Progress Motors never came close to living up to its promise of economic democracy. Increased power for the workers was never on the company's real agenda. Management was after more power, not less, and QWL became a mechanism for increasing management control while at the same time disguising it. These were grave threats to the workers' solidarity and to the unity of their local and their union. These threats have not abated.

Universal Electric

Like its counterpart at Progress Motors, management at Universal Electric told the workers that QWL would give them a bigger "say" on the job. It promised that decisions would be made jointly and that the workers' knowledge and ideas for solving workplace problems would be welcomed and respected. Once again, according to management, QWL was to signal the beginning of a new, genuinely participatory system of labor-management relations.

As at Progress Motors, there was only one valid measure of progress along the road to economic democracy, and that was a genuine increase in worker power, the power of the majority in the plant. That would have entailed an increase in unity among the workers and a greater awareness of their collective interests. It would have required greater solidarity. As in the auto plant, that was not what happened.

Within the CDM groups there was an overall increase in cohesion. Almost everyone who was a member of a CDM team for any length of time reported that the training sessions and weekly meetings had helped them to get to know the members of the group better. At the same time, there was an overall decrease in cohesion in all three of the departments where CDM groups were set up. This was because of the poor relations between CDM team members and workers who were not on the teams. The major issue was whether the activities of the CDM groups led to the loss of jobs. The argument against QWL was that improvements in productivity led to fewer workers being needed to produce the same amount. The counter-argument was that improved productivity, either in the form of better quality or reduced costs of production, made the department better able to compete for sales, and that more sales implied more rather than fewer jobs. Shaken by the criticism, however, some teams formally agreed not to give management any information that might lead to labor time being saved. The criticism nevertheless remained.

There were other suspicions. Not a few workers wondered if the members of the CDM groups were trying to gain favors from management. Were they after promotions? Were they hoping to gain qualifications that would make management less likely to lay them off? Others were suspicious because they felt that the team members were secretive about their discussions. The workers who became CDM team coordinators were especially mistrusted, and it was widely remarked that even their clothing and way of speaking had become like managements's. For their part, CDM team members spoke of having to take "constant flak" from fellow workers because of these suspicions. In some cases, workers who had been friends for years stopped talking to each other.

It is difficult to know how far these suspicions were justified. However, it is true that problem-solving by at least two teams led to criticisms of workers who were not on the teams. Members of the CDM teams in one department also willingly supported the violation of seniority provisions: during a layoff they openly favored the retention of some low-seniority maintenance workers over those with more seniority on the grounds that those with less seniority were more competent. The implication of this view for solidarity between maintenance workers and production workers is obvious. Management, of course, saw it as an indication of the success of QWL.

Management also claimed that QWL reduced worker resistance, not just in the areas with CDM teams but elsewhere in the plant as well. Management considered the CDM teams to be one main reason for this; they considered the human relations approach to be another. The evidence for this claim was the decline in resistance itself. A plant manager illustrated how the workers became more cooperative, even as the company took their jobs away from them:

> We put a mechanized line in the Wiring Department and that eliminated twenty-six jobs. In the past this would have been done suddenly and then twenty-six layoff notices would have been given out. Instead, we told them what we were going to do. We told them how it would be accomplished, showed them as a group what the effect would be. Conventionally, the junior people would have gone onto the [new] line because there was no incentive pay [on the new jobs]. But in this case the more senior workers wanted the jobs—to identify with the new machinery and as a matter of faith in the business.

Although there were many layoffs, there was not a single walkout or work stoppage to protest them. Prior to the coming of QWL such protests would have been a certainty. Management also pointed out that several influential militants became much more compliant after they joined the CDM groups.

Of course, QWL was not the only damper on worker militancy and solidarity at Universal Electric. Massive and ongoing layoffs were another. Job insecurity in the midst of hard times has rarely inspired great worker resistance, certainly not among workers with an average age of about fifty, and about twenty-five years of service with the company. These long-service workers had had more time to adapt to their jobs—militants did not usually last that long. Furthermore, those who remained tended to have better jobs, and jobs that by their nature placed them in a more cooperative relationship with management. Finally, many of these long-service employees were desperately trying to hold on until they qualified for company pensions.

For these reasons, QWL was not the only factor reducing the workers' resistance. At the same time, management was confident that QWL was an important contributor to its gaining an increased measure of control over the workers.

As at Progress Motors, QWL at Universal Electric also posed a threat to the union leadership. There were five unions in the plant, one representing the production workers, the other four representing salaried white-collar workers. Two of the five— the production workers' union and the main white-collar union—were far larger than the rest, and they were the only two that played a major role in relation to QWL. It is therefore the impact of QWL on the leadership of these two unions that is considered here.

Of the two, QWL damaged the leadership of the salaried workers' union more, but that damage was still not substantial. Unlike the leadership of the blue-collar union, the leadership of the white-collar union supported QWL, and some of its members took a very active role in the CDM groups. As a result, some of the members, who believed that QWL led to a union-management relationship that was far too cozy, were openly critical of their leaders. This is probably one reason why the union leader most supportive of QWL lost votes in the election that followed the introduction of the CDM teams. Nevertheless, he won, and a majority of his constituents continued to support the program.

In addition, the international leadership of the union endorsed QWL, and this helped to dispel some of the criticism directed against its supporters at the local level.

By contrast, both the local and national leadership of the production workers' union opposed QWL from the beginning, and only four stewards openly supported the CDM program. One of these withdrew early on from the training program, arguing that it had little to offer workers, while two others subsequently lost office. This left only one steward as an active member of a CDM group. With this sole exception, the local leadership was united on the issue and there is no evidence that QWL created serious internal divisions on the matter.

By refusing to cooperate in setting up QWL, the local union saved itself from the internal dissension that would have followed when QWL failed to live up to its promises. The danger was minimized because very few workers thought that QWL or any other change could do much to save their jobs. (The axe of unemployment intimidates workers best when there is some reasonable chance it will not fall anyway!) So if QWL posed less of a threat to union leaders in this plant than in the auto plant, it was largely because the workers realized that the future of the plant was so dismal that no union policy would make much difference. Another reason QWL was less harmful here was that management was less inclined to incite the CDM groups against the stewards, in part because the stewards often had the best verbal, mathematical, and analytical skills—skills that were at a premium in the CDM teams.

If Universal Electric had been miraculously saved from the economic scrapheap, then it seems likely that here too QWL would have been used to undermine the collective bargaining process and the union as a whole. The danger would have been that the CDM groups, like the quality boosters, would become substitutes for collective bargaining procedures and that deals between Mister-Nice-Guy supervisors and workers would be used to get around the grievance process. As at Progress Motors, the facade of "one big happy family" would begin to blind the workers to their adversarial relationship to management, and the union would become redundant. In the end, however, the shutdown of the plant intervened.

Conclusion

The QWL programs in both plants failed to live up to the key promises that the managers and consultants had made to the workers and their unions. Most jobs did not get better, job security did not improve, and the workers had no real say about their working lives. Instead, most of the jobs in both plants remained the same; some became considerably worse. At Progress Motors, job security did not improve; at Universal Electric, it was lost entirely; and in both cases the workers' efforts, where they had any discernible impact at all, actually contributed to job loss. Finally, instead of paving the way toward industrial democracy, QWL undermined the workers' already vulnerable position, enhancing management domination both on the job and at the bargaining table. Both programs helped management to weaken worker solidarity and militancy, threaten the legitimacy and unity of union leadership, and sow doubts among the members about the value of trade unionism itself.

These contrasts between the promises and realities of QWL are stark, but they do not justify any condemnation of the workers and union leaders who believed in QWL and supported it. Most of them hoped that maybe, just maybe, after all these years they could do something to improve their working lives. They hoped QWL would mean simple respect and greater dignity on the job, and that the programs would afford them relief from the haunting fear of unemployment. Although skeptical, several even shared a vision that some day workers and managers would be equal.

Most of them felt that they had no real choice. Management and the consultants and their own experience taught them, in effect, that the logic of the market was insurmountable, and that they and their fellow workers therefore had but two options: either participate in QWL or their company's competitors would take their jobs.

Most believed they had nothing to lose by becoming involved. Unfortunately, they were wrong, and those who were the strongest believers often lost the most.

5
Extending the Frontiers of Management Control

In marked contrast to the assurance of the consultants, the quality of working life (QWL) programs at Progress Motors and Universal Electric were not "win-win" situations benefiting both management and labor. Instead, while they were a source of major gains for management, the programs were clearly detrimental to the workers and their unions. This was no accident. Each of these programs was an integral part of a management strategy to increase control over a labor process that was being altered by new competitive pressures and technological innovations. Partly because of the way the programs were advertised, and partly because they represented a turning away from the previous harsher style of management control, they appeared to workers as something new and potentially beneficial. And, in a limited sense, they were.

Consider the previous style of management control at Progress Motors. Throughout most of the plant's history, relations between workers and management had been hostile. Like workers throughout the industry, workers in this plant had shown great courage and determination in resisting aggressive management policies, both through legal strikes and direct action, including sabotage, walkouts, sit-downs, slowdowns, concerted absenteeism, and the like. In addition to the struggle for better economic conditions, much of this resistance had been in response to extremely tight and obvious management control. The assembly line itself was the most fundamental aspect of this control—acting as an impersonal management agent, setting the pace of work. Also fundamental to management control and worker resistance was a highly detailed system for defining and classifying jobs, which set out exactly how each task was to be done, often to the split second, as well as specifying each worker's wages, bumping rights, and several other conditions of employment. Worker resistance was also a response to the close and sometimes harsh practices of line supervisors, general supervisors, and others (who were themselves directed from above).

Management's general goal had not been to eliminate resistance but to contain it, channel it, and use it to advantage. Throughout most of the postwar period, worker resistance was contained in large measure through collective bribery: contracts negotiated by the UAW set the standard for organized labor as a whole, not only in terms of wages but in benefits as well. The UAW also pioneered the introduction of such collective-bargaining innovations as cost-of-living adjustment (COLA) escalators, supplemental unemployment benefits, paid personal holidays, and much else. A great deal of worker resistance that could not be bought off was channeled into controlled conflict, either through formal strikes, which often acted as safety valves for discontent, or through step-by-step grievance procedures. With the union legally bound by the contract's no-strike clause to abide by the official grievance procedures, much of the day-to-day conflict was removed from the shop floor into management's offices, where it could be disposed of in a quasi-legal fashion that was beyond the control of those workers most directly affected. It often took months and even years before grievances were resolved—delays that were designed to be extended cooling-off periods.

Conflicts that were not channeled into the grievance procedure also often worked to management's advantage. Periodic direct action, such as work stoppages by small work groups, served as a safety valve for pent-up frustrations arising from the nature of the work and the harsh exercise of supervisory power. Such small-scale skirmishes also operated as an "early warning" system for supervisors, alerting them to the location and nature of discontent, and giving them an opportunity to identify militants and to mete out exemplary punishment, as well as to remind other workers of their vulnerability to firing and suspension. A policy of "progressive discipline," involving cumulatively harsher penalties for repeat offenders, helped management check the development of militant leadership on the shop floor.

Despite the advantages, there were considerable costs associated with this kind of industrial relations. These included high rates of absenteeism, turnover, alcoholism, and drug abuse, together with the costs incurred through the use of the grievance procedure. The costs of oversupervision were also large. Not least in importance, the job classification system was too rigid to permit flexible adaptation to changing technology, skill requirements, and levels of product demand. At Progress Motors, it was only the company's oligopolistic market position that enabled it to absorb these costs without squeezing profit margins, in part because they were passed along to consumers as price increases.

However, during the oil crisis of the 1970s and the recession of the early 1980s the company's ability to recover such costs was shaken by powerful new economic forces. Chief among them was a slump in demand, an enormous and sustained decline in sales greater than that in other industries, partly because of the high cost of cars. In addition, Asian competitors, with major cost advantages, were moving into many of the firm's traditional markets. A rapid shift in consumer taste toward smaller, more fuel-efficient cars was also cutting into sales. In addition, Progress Motors was faced with a not-inaccurate reputation for overpriced, poor-quality products, which it was trying to overcome through costly advertising campaigns. It was also saddled with an old plant and outdated machinery at a time of rapid technological change in the industry. In order to remain competitive in an industry that was becoming increasingly global in production, massive new investment was required.

For all these reasons, the company faced a crisis of profitability, and it was this crisis that underlay the desire to change the

system of industrial relations. There was also a pointed awareness that the company's principal overseas competitors were
getting along far better with their unionized workers. Such
success attracted emulation.

The benefits management derived from its old system of
control over its workers had reached their limit, yet there
remained a domain of potential productivity that had not been
tapped, a domain that contained the intimate knowledge that
the workers had of their tools and the products they made with
those tools. It included the ability to report or not to report, to
rectify or not to rectify, a host of production problems, and the
ability to make an effort that simply could not be coerced. This
domain lay along management's "last frontier" of control over
the workers, and at its center was the main day-to-day
battleground between labor and management—the relationship between workers and front-line supervisors. Younger,
generally more sophisticated, managers, especially those who
had been exposed to the latest business school industrial-psy-
chology courses, knew that this frontier could only be crossed
with the *voluntary* cooperation of the workers.

Many managers were especially concerned that the previous
emphasis on rigid workplace rules and narrow job descriptions
and training was counterproductive to the development of a
more informally coordinated, broadly trained workforce that
could be shifted quickly and efficiently between jobs in line with
rapid adjustments in production and with the capabilities of the
new microelectronic and robotic technologies. The traditional
workplace controls were also deemed inconsistent with the
preference for a new system of quality control in which workers
were to be charged with inspecting the quality of their own
work.

This was not the only rationale for encouraging the workers'
voluntary cooperation. Management also hoped that this cooperation would carry over into an acceptance of wage and benefit
cuts in contract bargaining, as well as a tolerance for the
"outsourcing" (importing) of nonunion parts, the contracting out
of services to nonunion labor, and the elimination of production

jobs through various means. (In this respect it is interesting to note that in 1981 General Motors circulated a confidential memo among its executives throughout North America encouraging them to use QWL programs to convince workers that their union's collective-bargaining demands were dangerous to the economic health of the company.) Management was also interested in promoting QWL as part of a public relations campaign to reinforce public antipathy toward adversarial unionism and, at the same time, to promote the image of its cars and trucks as high quality products. For management at Progress Motors, QWL was to be an antidote to all these problems.

A similar set of problems with the traditional management-control strategy underlay the introduction of QWL at Universal Electric. There too management had relied primarily on overt coercion by supervisors and on a delay-ridden grievance process. The costs were similar: work stoppages, bitter strikes, high rates of employee absenteeism and turnover, widespread alcohol abuse, and a large and expensive contingent of first-line supervisors whose main role was to maintain order.

As at Progress Motors, the enormous size and financial strength of the company relative to most of its competitors made these costs bearable. Then came the hard years of the 1970s and 1980s. Profit rates fell as demand for many of the firm's products plummeted. As foreign firms closed the technological lead Universal had enjoyed, they took large chunks of its market in several product areas. In response, Universal management made major changes in its corporate structure, selling off old plants, buying new ones, developing "high-tech" investments to replace more traditional labor-intensive ones, and making joint-production alliances with some of its foreign competitors. Along with this, Universal embarked on a long-term strategy to change its system of labor relations, a strategy that included shutting down several of its unionized plants and "running away" to produce in nonunion areas. Central to this change in strategy was QWL.

Management at Universal was pursuing both short-term and long-term goals by introducing the CDM program at the plant. According to internal management memoranda, the immediate goal was to use the program as a vehicle "to introduce change so that individuals respond to the need to accept it." In other words, the objective was to push through productivity increases without creating resistance. According to another internal document, management's longer-term goal was to incorporate lessons gained from the program into "a package of learning exercises" that would be used by others. The experiments at Universal were to become part of a broader corporate labor relations strategy that was to be applied in other plants in the United States and Canada. Management hoped that in future years a full-fledged QWL program would deliver an explosion of productivity: the plan was that if management provided the planning and necessary investment, the workers would deliver the additional competitive edge. Meanwhile, Universal Electric served as a valuable experimental site, with workers as the QWL guinea pigs.

In both plants the transition from one style of management control to another was accomplished by offering the programs to workers and union leaders as strictly limited and quite formal arrangements. In practice, however, this applied only to the first phase of what was in fact a much more ambitious hidden agenda according to which incremental changes would eventually compel the workers and their union to accept wholesale alterations both on the job and in the entire collective-bargaining process. At Universal Electric, the workers thought they were cooperating with a program that would save their jobs, not one that would provide management with experience to use elsewhere. Nor did they understand that "cooperative decision-making" (CDM) was only one change among others, including the training of their supervisors in more subtle control techniques.

Management had grander ambitions at Progress Motors as

well. QWL innovations were first presented to union leaders as a specific program to be developed within definite structures: the steering committee, with its equal numbers from each side, and its veto powers; and the pilot projects themselves, with their project committees subordinated to the steering committee. Partly because this was the way QWL was defined for them, and partly because these were the elements that gave them a formal role, most union leaders at Progress Motors thought this was the essence of QWL. To the extent that they were aware of the new supervisory style, the new employee involvement activities, and the quality-booster program, they regarded them as quite separate innovations. This distinction—between the original QWL program and the later additions—was asserted publically by management as well; it was not until later that it became clear to the workers and the union that all of these elements were part of a single management-dominated process.

One major difference between QWL as it was first presented to the steering committee and the reality that it later came to be centered on the issue of official union participation. If the definitive goal of QWL had been to encourage a genuine partnership between the union and management, it would certainly have made sense to think of it as a carefully delimited program agreed to by both. However, in both of these plants (and elsewhere as well), union cooperation was not really necessary; on the contrary, most QWL programs are set up to ward off unions. Although it is true that at Progress Motors management preferred to implement the QWL program with union support, union collaboration was simply an important way to ease QWL onto the plant floor. Such support was readily discarded once management had accomplished this objective. Even when the steering committee put the pilot projects on hold, the aura of union cooperation with management remained, giving QWL a legitimacy it would not otherwise have had. Without this highly visible collaboration on the part of the union, many workers would have regarded these innovations as just another gimmick to increase management control, especially since labor-management relations in the plant had long been antagonistic. With union cooperation, then, management was able to set up the first phases of QWL, and this beginning provided momentum for later phases.

It was alongside the pilot projects that management introduced most of its human relations innovations. Although these changes were implemented solely by the company, they were not questioned by the workers, partly because of the initially positive experience of the pilot projects. By the time the projects became a source of frustration, industrial relations had eased considerably. Even after contract negotiations, which involved union concessions, management was able to introduce the booster program without significant opposition from the workers or the union.

Somewhat surprisingly, management at Progress Motors later argued that the employee-involvement activities and the quality-booster program were not QWL programs because they involved actual changes in the organization of work. Management claimed that true QWL, as in the case of the pilot projects, concerned environmental changes. This distinction was precisely the opposite of that made in the consultants' QWL literature, which stated that the definitive characteristic of "true" or "genuine" QWL was the introduction of basic changes in the organization of work, and which promised better jobs as a result.

Management was admittedly much happier with the employee involvement activities and the quality booster program than it had been with the pilot projects. One senior manager was emphatic in his judgment that "the employee-involvement actions in the plant have done more for the plant than the QWL [pilot] projects ever did." By this time, the company was prepared to weather opposition to QWL in any form.

At Universal Electric, in contrast, management was less successful at gaining the cooperation of the production workers' union. This meant that QWL had less legitimacy with many of the workers right from the start. Nevertheless, management did get the support of the white-collar workers' union, which provided some basis for claiming that QWL was part of a union-management partnership. In the beginning, management relied on QWL coordinators chosen from the ranks of the workers. Later on, once an atmosphere of cooperation had been established, management took direct control of the CDM teams. As at Progress Motors, the fact that management was in the driver's seat became apparent only after the QWL program was well under way.

The New Management-Control Strategy

In retrospect, it is clear that despite the differences between the programs, each was a management-control strategy containing the same four principal components. The first was *the controlled delegation of authority to selected workers*. The prime example of this was the transfer of authority to those individuals management regarded as natural leaders: the CDM team coordinators at Universal, and the project committee representatives and quality boosters at Progress Motors. By taking on some of management's *authority,* these workers accepted a gift that was subject to managerial veto and could be taken away at any moment. This was not the same thing, then, as workers taking some of management's *power*. Dependent on management in order to perform their new duties, these workers served as an extension of supervision.

This delegated authority was applicable to a very restricted range of decisions, principally those involving immediate, day-to-day job matters. Thus the workers in the pilot projects and the CDM teams were more than ever involved in detailed decisions about their work, including such things as the provision of tools, the maintenance of machines, housekeeping practices, procedures for the allocation and cleaning of work clothing, and so on. A similar set of concerns, the front-line supervisor's old donkey work, defined the range of authority delegated to the quality boosters. Management had decided on the framework within which these details were to be worked out.

Such delegation of authority encouraged workers in a way of thinking that was designed to implant management's own criteria of decision-making. This was most explicit in the CDM teams where, under the guise of "problem-solving," workers were taught to make decisions that were consistent with management's productivity goals. The same management criteria were implanted more subtly in the pilot projects in the auto plant. The results took a thousand forms. To one autoworker it meant that "you could cut down on the misuse of equipment and materials because guys would take pride in their work." To another it meant "little things": "If a screw falls out that's not part of my job, I fix it anyway." To another it meant simply that "the employee feels like he's doing something." And in both plants management hoped that management-oriented workers would become a "union within a union," undermining the local from within.

Management also knew that workers who were conditioned to think like managers and to police themselves could save the company a lot of money. Such conditioning could eliminate much of the need for front-line supervisors. In place of the costs of coercion, especially the costs of oversupervision, and the union grievance procedure, management was eager to install worker self-regulation. That, in its most concise form, is what QWL meant to management.

A second component found in both control strategies was management's *improved access to workers' skills and knowledge about their jobs.* The skills management sought access to included a remnant of those skills that had once been the property of craft workers (before management de-skilled their labor). Even though the workers themselves often vastly undervalued its importance, this remnant of these skills was significant in both plants. Management also wanted the knowledge that was embodied in the informal know-how that the workers used every day to make their work lives more pleasant, to make their jobs easier, to create a safer, healthier workplace, to resist speedups and job elimination, to defend their dignity against harassment—and to get their work done. Without these skills, in fact, production would have stopped. For obvious reasons, the workers usually hid such informal skills and know-how from their bosses; for equally obvious reasons, their bosses stood to gain a great deal from access to this information.

One of management's main ways of obtaining this knowledge at Progress Motors was through the project committees in Paint and Trim, through the formal and informal canvassing these committees did in order to gather workers' ideas and suggestions for improvements in the zones. A more important access point was the booster program, where management used the boosters themselves as channels of information. The various mechanisms of consultation between management and workers served the same purpose. (This suddenly became clear to one worker when a manager praised him for his attention to "details" and told him that now "we [management] have better ideas on how jobs should be run.")

At Universal Electric, the problem-solving in the CDM meetings explicitly called on workers to divulge their know-how on behalf of productivity improvements. Plant managers also had access to the workers' skills and knowledge through their close relationship with the CDM coordinators, and through the various human relations contacts supervisors cultivated with the workers.

The third component of this management-control strategy was *the promotion of work-group identity*. Both Progress Motors and Universal Electric knew that the key to enlisting the voluntary cooperation of the workers depended on turning the cooperation among workers within their work groups into cooperation with management. Management also knew that such cooperation could not be guaranteed by any agreement with the union leadership, which was far too removed from day-to-day activities on the job. Nor could such cooperation be effectively achieved on a one-to-one basis between supervisors and individual workers: this would have been too time-consuming and too costly. In both plants, management was also aware that the center of worker resistance lay in the work groups. For all these reasons, management therefore preferred a strategy that attached its goals for a certain quality standard, a certain level of production, and so on, to strong pro-management work-group identities.

In an important sense, the promotion of management-oriented work groups was directly related to the various human relations innovations, especially the front-line supervisors' softer style. It was also strongly related to the previously discussed first component: the delegation of low-level authority to selected workers. Unionists in both plants considered an increase in work-group identity and cohesion a good thing, largely because they equated it with mutual aid and "getting along"—with the general work culture of solidarity. Traditionally, a strong work-group identity did mean worker solidarity. However, once this was shaped by management, it became the exact opposite. Instead of solidarity, work-group identity led to "teams" of workers competing with each other or being drawn into productivity races between shifts or departments. It led to workers in the same work group pressuring each other to comply with management norms of cooperation. Such peer pressure at times bordered on vendettas against those who could not or would not cooperate in speedups and the like: workers who were physically or mentally weaker than their peers, those with emotional problems or drug dependencies, and, of course, those who were militant. (Since it was dehumanized working conditions that contributed to the health problems of the workers, the bitter irony was that QWL not only left the dehumanization essentially intact—or even worsened it—but that it encouraged its victims to blame, and punish, each other.)

In the pilot projects in the car plant, the focus of work-group identity was the entire zone, comprising twenty, thirty, or more workers; in the booster program it was a smaller group of eight or ten workers. This was an optimal size for sustaining cohesion through continuous face-to-face interaction. For this reason, the personal influence of the boosters was superior to the work of the project committees as a stimulus to work-group identity. The CDM teams fostered the same work-group identity-building at Universal Electric. After a false start, managers soon learned that such an identity could be oriented more effectively toward management if they expanded the CDM teams to bring the workers into close association with "resource" people who identified with management objectives. Management also devoted special attention to team members so that these workers would think of themselves as collectively "special." Executives at Universal hoped that this kind of group identity would lead to lower absenteeism, improved inventory control, and reduced job-related inefficiency.

At Progress Motors, management further reinforced work-group identification by supplying separate eating and relaxation areas, by painting different colors on the walls of each group's work area, and so on. In both plants, group identity was also strengthened in the training and orientation sessions. The promotion of such group identity was meant to reduce genuine solidarity and to assist management in tapping the benefits of group pressure. To the extent that such group conformity encouraged productivity rather than resistance, the benefits for management were clear.

The fourth and final component of both of these management-control strategies was *the forging of a stronger identification between the workers and the product they produced* (or at least that portion of it that a particular group worked on). Management promoted this product identification by promising that QWL would satisfy a work ethic that, in both plants, had been frustrated by management's own long-standing preference for quantity over quality in production. Management in both plants also promoted this identification by showing the workers how their jobs fit into the production process in their own area and the plant as a whole.

A more compelling dimension of this attempt was the emphasis management gave to the argument that improvements in product quality would shore up job security. It will be remembered that management at Progress Motors held a QWL orientation session for thousands of workers who returned after a long layoff. The workers were shown a film whose main theme was that mounting foreign competition was the supreme threat to the future of both the company and the workers. The same theme was contained in the plant manager's invitation to compare the quality of the plant's products with those made by these same Asian and European competitors. In these ways workers were encouraged to associate their support for the plant's products with feelings of patriotism—feelings that in some cases fed into racist attitudes, especially toward workers of Asian origin. To the extent that such conditioning took hold, the workers became increasingly divided along lines of race and ethnicity. Because the film also implied that foreign workers were happy to work harder for less, it reinforced the view that the workers at Progress were somehow responsible for the company's crisis of profitability. So, on top of everything else, they blamed themselves. The immediate result of the orientation program was that the productivity went "way up."

The QWL program at Progress Motors promoted product identification in other ways. Job rotation gave the workers a better understanding of how their jobs fit into the making of the product and a greater sense of involvement with other aspects of the production process. The project committees' efforts in Trim to allocate work loads more equally also fostered this sense of identification with jobs other than one's own, as did consultations about changes in product design and work setups, since maintaining quality standards was their primary responsibility. The promotion of product identification was also part of the quality boosters' role, but the most clear-cut aspect of this identity-creation process in the auto plant was worker involvement in the multimillion-dollar advertising campaign, which focused on the workers' pride in the quality of the products manufactured at Progress Motors.

At Universal Electric, management promoted worker identification with the products of their labor primarily through the CDM teams. In addition to production workers, the teams included those technical and managerial personnel who were responsible for the products that the team was making. The team was thus defined by the product. As one Universal executive explained, the development of this product identification was consciously tied to CDM problem-solving techniques: "We had to find a way to marry that [work group] identity with the need to resolve problems in the area," he explained. "In other words, we had to expand the employees' concept of what was their stake in the area as a whole." This was part of the reason why CDM focused on the need to understand how the whole product was produced.

These four major components—delegating limited authority to a few workers, improving access to the workers' knowledge, and getting workers to identify more closely with the work group and the product—were characteristic of QWL in both plants. Each component served specific management objectives, which meshed with the overall goal of increasing management power over the workers. The implementation of each component depended on the same management power being disguised, at least in part, as an improvement in the quality of working life. Yet, all along, at both Progress Motors and Universal Electric, the actual quality of working life was subordinated to the overriding goal of greater profits. This was the real nature of the "cooperative" "win-win" system of labor-management relations in these plants.

6

Can QWL Lead to Workers' Control?

That these programs were subtle strategies to increase management control is clear. At the same time, it is arguable that
management was being too clever by half, and that in the longer
run QWL might provide workers with a vehicle for increasing
their power in the workplace. The rationale for this argument
stems from the premise that QWL is central to a new kind of
industrial relations, one that offers a far broader scope for
change in the workplace than the industrial relations systems
currently in force in the United States and Canada.

It is a fundamental characteristic of conventional postwar
collective bargaining in North America that "money issues"
(wages and fringe benefits) have, until recently, almost always
been the top priority. Any questioning of "management's rights"
to make decisions about production—and hence working life—
has normally been taboo. Union leaders have generally respected this taboo, partly because money issues have usually been
the membership's chief concern. More fundamentally, however,
both union leaders and members have gone along because they
have had little choice: whereas employers in the postwar period
have commonly been prepared to discuss concessions around
pay and fringe benefits, they have been adamantly opposed to
conceding any of their power. QWL is supposed to change this:
for the first time, control issues are supposed to be on the
negotiating table. And certainly workers welcome this promise:
so many of the issues that are now so pressing for workers—
issues such as job security, technological change, health and

safety, and the contracting out of work to non-union firms—are directly or indirectly related to rights over the control of production that have traditionally been exclusive to management.

If management were willing to share power with workers, the implications for the workplace—and for society generally—would be potentially enormous. A vast literature about workers' control testifies to this, showing that greater powers of decision-making at work lead to significant improvement in workers' health, both mental and physical. These expanded decision-making powers have also been shown to carry over into life outside work, particularly in the form of greater sociability and in more frequent and meaningful participation in politics.

Finally, from the union point of view, more meaningful decision-making by workers on the job may help to revitalize the labor movement. If the enforced habits of obedience at work give way to a new assertiveness and self-confidence, this could encourage greater member participation in, and control of, unions—and this in turn could lead to demands for further inroads into "management's rights."

The broader implications of worker control, then, are that greater powers of decision-making on the job can help to develop a more genuinely democratic society. Such a society would be based on more and better participation by the "average" citizen than is possible in today's spectator sport of electoral politics. Economic democracy would complement and vastly enhance the narrow political democracy that we now know.

The social benefits for broader worker participation in the workplace are therefore potentially huge. This vision is not the cardinal issue, however. Instead, the paramount question, on which all other questions hinge, is whether the new industrial relations can or will lead in this direction. More specifically, can QWL qualify as a genuine form of worker participation? Should QWL be regarded as a seed from which democracy in the workplace, the union, and the society can grow?

Certainly there is an abstract logic according to which it has been argued that QWL could lead in the direction of greater worker control: if QWL were associated with greater job security and increased worker identification with the labor process, then the quite limited worker participation found in the typical QWL program might whet workers' appetite for more power, to the point where real worker control could emerge. Consider Universal Electric, for example. It is possible to imagine the CDM teams broadening the range of their decision-making as connections developed between the issues they were working on and issues previously outside their jurisdiction. Indeed, workers in some CDM groups actually did begin to make suggestions that affected more than their own work. Sooner or later, it is also likely that the CDM teams would have realized that the problems they were asked to solve were inseparable from policies regarding personnel selection and training, product design, the introduction of new technology, the scheduling of production, and so on. In addition, if workers were able to build more skills into their jobs, this might have become the basis for a new sense of competence and confidence, something that might eventually have encouraged them to demand still more control over their work and their lives.

This is only an imagined scenario, however. In practice, there were a number of built-in safeguards against this happening, safeguards so compelling that in the end QWL could pose no challenge to management control. In fact, quite the reverse was true: the more the union and the workers cooperated with QWL, the *less* management had to control the workers and their union by other means. Indeed workers who were suspicious of QWL were often not critical enough: they tended to underestimate the control aspect and see QWL almost exclusively in terms of its direct economic benefits for management. For example, some workers in both plants argued that QWL was simply a bargain-basement suggestion box: management got to "pick the workers' brains" for the price of an annual steak dinner. This kind of hard-nosed dollars-and-cents perspective—which was accurate as far as it went—blinded the workers to the control dimension, something that was far more important to management in the long run than the immediate economic payoff.

The truth is that management could well have afforded greater worker participation without forfeiting any significant "management rights" over either workers or the production process. Considering the limited effectiveness of worker resistance and the workers' very profound and rational fear of unemployment, together with the absence of any realistic vision of what workers' control might mean to them (even if they had the power to achieve it), it becomes clear that any amount of worker participation could only result in more management control, not less. There is no evidence that any worker ever thought that QWL would lead to genuine workers' control, or that any wanted it. What they aspired to was not autonomous working-class power, but a certain reciprocity in their relations with management, an opportunity for both sides to cooperate, to do good quality work, and to work efficiently. Given both the objective power relations and the workers' aspirations, one can only conclude that the QWL programs in these plants were highly unlikely candidates for *any* challenge to management control.

At Universal Electric, management's originally stated intention was that the CDM teams would be "self-managed." Having a QWL consultant initiate the program would relieve management of the job of either setting up or running the groups directly. He was to play a mediating role between workers and management. In practice, however, the QWL consultant was not at all neutral, since he was an agent of management—hired by management, paid by management, and with no authority independent of management.

After the consultant left, the workers ran most of the CDM teams—but not exactly as they wished. Instead, through a variety of direct and indirect mechanisms, management was able to control the contours—if not the details—of decision-making in the groups, and even to increase its control. Management controlled the pace at which the CDM teams expanded and selected the departments in which they were set up. It controlled the decision-making in the groups themselves by ensuring that the workers followed procedures that were management-oriented and based on specific management criteria. It also controlled the selection of problems to be solved, which were restricted to the areas that the CDM teams worked in, and could only be implemented with the limited resources management made available. It decided which of the teams' solutions would be implemented and which would not. The CDM teams "don't bring anything back that's stupid," a supervisor explained. "They know damn well if I just look at it [and don't act on it], that's as far as it's gonna go." And management had a total monopoly on the power of the purse. While a Universal Electric supervisor, for example, might have had the authority to spend up to $500 at his personal discretion, the manager of shop operations up to $10,000, and the plant manager up to $50,000, the CDM teams did not have the authority to spend a single cent!

The best indication of the degree to which management controlled QWL was that it rarely had to put its foot down and refuse a suggestion. Management was able to shape the decision-making process to such an extent that vetoes were unnecessary. This was not only because management laid down the criteria, but because management influenced members of the groups. Consider who the CDM team members were: in addition to production workers, there were engineers and other technical-resource people—people who were normally well attuned to what management wanted. And the entire problem-solving process was highly dependent on their expertise.

Next, look at the production workers. Included among them were quality-control inspectors and lead hands who had been trained in courses for supervisors. Then there were the CDM team coordinators. While not all of these were chosen by management, all were dependent on management, were given extra pay by management, were regularly advised by management, were trained and encouraged by management, and in one or two cases were even promoted off the shop floor by management.

Management further ensured its control of the teams by keeping them apart. The teams in different departments were given very few opportunities to get together and develop a network that might reduce their isolation. (It was, after all, the departments' relative isolation that made them attractive as places to set up CDM teams in the first place.)

Finally, management, subtly and not so subtly, intervened in group decision-making. The more subtle way was to plant an agent in a team. "We monitored [the CDM teams] very closely," one plant manager explained, "but left them to their own devices. I would plant one of my confidants in the group and he would egg people on in the direction I wanted." These agents also discouraged more independent-minded workers from continuing to participate. Another manager explained how this was accomplished: "You get somebody who can put them [the independent ones] down and you get dropouts for that reason." When this kind of tactic failed to work, management turned to less subtle methods. For example, as one company executive reported, although the change in the composition of the teams in the Transformer Department was highly unpopular, management unilaterally "railroaded it through after the initial protests of the group."

So the so-called self-managed CDM teams were nothing of the sort, and there is no reason to believe that they could break away from such near total management control. The same is true of management control of the QWL projects in the Trim and Paint zones at Progress Motors. There was never any basis for worker autonomy, either through the project committees or through the steering committee. The project committees had no power to implement anything that had not been approved by the steering committee, and the union had no real power on the steering committee. Although the union had voting parity with management, this was irrelevant, a mere illusion of power, since management always had the final say about whether money would be spent. The only option the union had was to withdraw from the steering committee, but that was an empty gesture because management was already employing its own much broader QWL strategy in which the union had no role.

The quality boosters, as we have seen, were similarly powerless. Their authority was even more narrowly circumscribed than that of front-line supervisors. If anything, their privileges relative to other workers made them less inclined than their fellows to resist management.

For all these reasons, the QWL programs in both plants were not an opening toward industrial democracy but rather a move away from it. As management clearly intended, QWL enhanced its control. Of course, this did not mean that the increase in management power was transparent. Quite the reverse. If management had been too obvious in exercising its will, or too heavy-handed, it would have gone against the grain of QWL. The whole point of QWL was for management to go past the frontiers marking the limits of what could be achieved through coercion. QWL extended these boundaries precisely to the degree that management was able to exercise power while appearing to do what the workers wanted.

It is not difficult to understand that those workers who continued to serve on the project committees at Progress Motors and the CDM teams at Universal Electric did so primarily because they felt that "soft" management was an improvement over "hard" management. In both plants, the workers appreciated those supervisors and managers who became more approachable and down-to-earth, who seemed more friendly and trustworthy. In some cases, this less authoritarian management style was a source of improved self-esteem for the workers. For other workers, and for some union leaders, it provided a sense of power. But these feelings of equality and power were a delusion. What counted in the end was not the power that the workers and their union *felt,* but their real power to make decisions.

Notwithstanding the assurances of consultants and managers that workers would have a bigger say, and despite the hopes of those who looked forward to a more participatory workplace, the QWL programs in these plants could not have resulted in anything but an increase in management control. As long as management power so clearly prevailed, right from the start, it would have been naive to anticipate that anything else could have happened. Why would management ever want to forfeit real control to the workers? After all, the control of workers is what management is all about, and no management that wanted to continue to *be* management would ever voluntarily give up its power. Management recognizes this; so do most workers. The astonishing thing is that anyone who was experienced in the modern worlds of work would suggest—or believe—anything to the contrary.

The Origins of QWL

Once it is clear the QWL does not mean what its promoters say it means (better jobs, more job security, and equal say for workers), it also becomes clear that there is very little that is new about QWL. Certainly other kinds of management control, such as simple coercion and "scientific management" (whereby managers de-skill jobs, leaving workers with hyper-simplified tasks involving little or no personal discretion), have long been—and continue to be—more central to management power, but the repertoire of sophisticated managers has very often been supplemented by much softer approaches. Indeed, various kinds of managerial paternalism directed toward the adjustment of workers to the labor process are as old as the factory system. QWL is a variant on these approaches but it can be more specifically traced, at least in part, to company unionism before and after World War I and to the Human Relations school of management, which began during the 1920s.

As with QWL today, management's interest in tame unions and in the Human Relations approach arose in the midst of intense changes in the workplace. After the 1870s, workplace organization and industrial relations throughout the United States and Canada, but especially in the industrial heartland of the U.S. northeast, underwent the beginnings of a major transition away from traditional small-scale manufacture toward modern mass industry. As firms grew larger and more complex, relations between workers and their employers became increasingly impersonal. In many of the major manufacturing industries, management adopted a policy of de-skilling jobs and employing cheaper semiskilled or unskilled labor, thereby undermining the traditional job controls of craft workers.

Although management regarded these sources of vast gains in productivity and profits as "progress," workers increasingly saw this new factory system as tyranny. Labor-management relations grew more and more hostile and even bloody. Many workers protested by quitting, and they resisted through sabotage, work stoppages, and the threat of unionism. Usually in alliance with courts and governments, companies frequently responded harshly, as they had for many years, quelling these strikes with blacklists, bullets, billy clubs, jail sentences, and deportations. Employers also took advantage of immigration policies to hire "green" immigrant labor as scabs to undermine worker solidarity.

Yet it was during these same years prior to and after World War I that many employers began to look seriously for other ways to solve their "labor problem." Afraid that the Bolshevik virus would cross the Atlantic, many became interested in the "human side of industry." This often meant that in addition to being denounced as lazy, uncivilized, incapable, and prone to violence, workers were considered "not as servants but as cooperators." Management became particularly concerned with workers' attitudes toward authority and work. Many said that they believed workers had a strong work ethic and wanted to contribute to production, and that they should be encouraged to cooperate with management.

Consistent with this view and with their anxiety to head off the creation of genuine unions, employers came up with a form of industrial partnership, an "American way" to deal with industrial unrest: they sponsored management-controlled company unions—called "works councils," "employee representation plans," and "industrial democracy." Often these were installed along with various company welfare measures, which the worker "representatives" helped to administer.

One of the best known of these company unions was the "Rockefeller Plan," devised by William Lyon Mackenzie King, who later became prime minister of Canada. (It was set up during World War I in the wake of management's hard approach to labor relations at the Colorado Fuel and Iron Company, an approach that had resulted in the infamous Ludlow Massacre in which miners and their families were shot and burned to death.) Like the QWL programs at Progress Motors and Universal Electric, and similar to the way other company unions are organized, the Rockefeller Plan provided for the election of worker representatives and for labor-management committees. Also akin to numerous QWL programs was the fact that neither the representatives nor the committees had any power to initiate changes without management consent. Finally, like QWL programs today, these schemes usually arose as management's response to a crisis. Normally they did not live much longer than the crisis that led to their creation.

It was also during these same years that management came under the influence of the then relatively new "sciences" of sociology and psychology, in the hope that they would identify the causes of worker discontent and specify remedies. This expectation marked the beginning of the Human Relations school of management. This approach grew out of a series of experiments begun by Elton Mayo at the Western Electric Company in Chicago in the late 1920s. Mayo's conclusions about the problems of conflict in the workplace gave birth to a new "science" of human relations in industry, designed to help administrative elites improve their own and workers' "social skills." The aim was to promote worker cooperation with management's productivity goals. This approach became highly influential, reinforcing the shift of managerial attention away from a preoccupation with coercion toward a greater concern with workplace culture, in particular with workers' attitudes and values. The hope was that the new social sciences would become allies of management by finding ways to bring workers' attitudes and values into line with the increasingly demanding requirements of mass production—without in any fundamental way changing the organization of work or the structure of power in the workplace.

Although the human relations exponents originally centered their attention on the psychology of individual workers, they soon broadened their focus and began to work on the sociology and psychology of small-group behavior. Whereas the orthodox management assumption had been that the main purpose of work groups was to subvert management objectives, the human relations experts concluded that work groups reflected a normal human need for sociability. Instead of suppressing work groups, employers were advised to channel them away from their attempts to frustrate management goals. The Human Relations approach also taught management to seek the collaboration of workers by consulting them about changes in working conditions. In addition, stress was placed on the need for a sense of group identification and peer group pressure as routes toward increasing productivity. Not surprisingly, it was during this period—the 1920s and 1930s—that the "family" metaphor became popular in industrial relations.

The personal qualities of natural leaders in the context of the group were also considered critical, and attempts were made to enlist the supervisors in this role through training in "social skills." Counseling to help workers adjust to their jobs, while at the same time keeping an eye out for discontent, was added to the other control mechanisms.

Another industrial relations scheme that is part of the background of QWL also gained prominence at this time: the Productivity Sharing Plan. Such plans normally combine some form of worker participation with collective rewards for the workers based on their contributions to productivity improvements. The best-known variant was created in the 1930s by Joe Scanlon, an accountant and labor official, in an attempt to save an ailing steel company. The Scanlon Plan provided group bonuses to workers in return for suggestions and work practices that reduced costs and increased productivity. In order to encourage additional worker participation, a network of labor-management committees in each department was set up. Representatives on these committees met regularly to discuss problems and voice the workers' ideas about how to make production more efficient. While these committees were empowered to implement certain kinds of suggestions on their own authority, proposals affecting a larger part of the enterprise or requiring greater funding were passed on to higher level committees, which evaluated them and made recommendations to management. Since the Scanlon Plan provided material incentives to *groups* of workers, pressures to speed up tended to come from fellow workers in the groups, thereby relieving management of some of the burden. Today, the Scanlon Plan is employed mainly by smaller firms in both union and nonunion situations.

The Rucker Plan is another kind of productivity-sharing plan that is common today. It is similar to the Scanlon Plan except that it has a more limited committee system. The IMPROSHARE (IMproved PROductivity through SHARing) Plan is also related to the Scanlon Plan, but it has less connection to QWL because it provides little or no employee participation.

QWL is also rooted in changes in industrial relations which took place during World War II. Under both the Canadian Industrial Production Cooperation Board and the U.S. War Production Board, thousands of joint labor-management shop committees were formed. Membership on these committees was voluntary but the labor representatives tended to be the official union leaders. With a view to increasing productivity, the committees met to discuss absenteeism, health and safety issues, personnel problems, and training requirements. The major contrast between this wartime innovation and contemporary QWL is that very few firms tried to get workers *directly* involved in discussing ways to increase efficiency. Furthermore, the jurisdiction of the committees was distinct from collective bargaining. Most of the cooperation underlying these committees stemmed from wartime patriotism, and most were disbanded after the war was over.

World War II brought with it another industrial relations legacy that is even more directly related to contemporary QWL, but one that is at the same time curiously roundabout. After the Japanese military was crushed in 1945, there was a subsequent, lesser known defeat, this time of organized labor. In the wake of prolonged, failed strikes, independent unions and the left wing of the Japanese labor movement were all but completely finished. With much of the Japanese working class demoralized and disorganized, legislation was introduced which engineered a fragmented, decentralized union structure focussed at the level of the individual firm. The consequence was a new industrial relations system based on company unions headed by management-sponsored labor "racketeers."

These company unions have endured as a pillar of the Japanese industrial relations system, although aside from systematically colluding with management they have hardly any role to play. A second pillar of modern Japanese industrial relations was erected after Japanese managers visited the United States. Looking for the sources of the military and industrial strength that had defeated Japan, they came upon the employee-team concept embodied in the Scanlon Plan and took it home. Thus it was that the legacy of worker participation schemes in North America contributed to the transplantation of the employee team concept to Japan. Given the weakness and disorganization of the Japanese labor movement and the presence of company unions, especially in the larger firms—where (in contrast to workers in small firms) employers often enjoy relatively high wages (including bonuses), fringe benefits, and, perhaps most importantly, considerable job security (for core workers, this means life-long employment)—the environment was highly receptive and the transplant took firm root.

By the 1960s, "quality control circles," based on small groups of workers headed by front-line supervisors—who were normally also the most experienced workers and leaders in the workplace—had been set up in thousands of workplaces in

Japan. An example is the Japanese post office, where this form of QWL began as a series of pilot projects in the early 1960s. One of the postal workers reported that after a nucleus of pro-management workers had been established, management set about reorganizing most of the jobs. This resulted in a protracted period of worker resistance that lasted throughout the 1970s and led management to introduce a new program based on the premise that people work harder when they feel they are responsible for what happens in their workplace and that they make sacrifices when they can attain their own "autonomous" purposes in their jobs.

According to this scheme, all of the postal workers were divided into groups of five to ten members and management asked each person to link his or her aim to that of the group. Efficiency was each group's "autonomous" task. Management appointed a leader for each group and encouraged this person to believe that he or she was special. Group discussions began with uncontroversial issues and then moved on to deal with how to increase efficiency, how to compete with other groups, and how to deal with workers who did not cooperate in furthering these objectives.

The great irony is that this Japanese emulation of North American industrial relations was re-imported by management in North America as the core feature of an attempt to emulate Japanese industrial relations. Having crossed the Pacific, the "Japanese model" meshed not only with the human relations tradition and company unionism but also with a renewed interest in "participative management" that had been taking place, especially in business schools, since the early 1960s. In 1960 the psychologist Douglas McGregor published *The Human Side of Enterprise,* a book that soon became enormously influential. McGregor recommended the Scanlon Plan as an example of excellent management and argued that because many workers' basic physical and safety needs were already satisfied, pay incentives were no longer as effective in increasing productivity. His famous "Theory Y" asserted that "external control and the threat of punishment are not the only means for bringing about effort toward organizational objectives." McGregor's thesis was complemented by the very popular work of another psychologist, Frederick Herzberg, who maintained that management should motivate workers through positive "satisfiers" rather than through traditional negative controls. Herzberg recommended that management remove some of the direct controls over workers while increasing their accountability. It was ideas such as these that were spreading rapidly among better educated managers while the Japanese model was taking hold in North America.

To varying degrees, the Japanese model also meshed with European work on the development of "sociotechnical" systems that were supposed to provide a balance between the technological "bones" and the human "flesh" of the production process. Much of the emphasis of this work was placed on increasing the authority of small groups of workers. The Japanese model also had affinities with certain aspects of "Organizational Development," an approach that emerged out of postwar research into the dynamics of small groups. Organizational Development, however, was clearly based on the adjustment of workers to production processes, while the production processes were considered more or less fixed.

As competition increased in the 1970s and 1980s, and as Japan's economy emerged to a position of startlingly rapid dominance, leading U.S. firms, including Lockheed, Honeywell, Ford, Westinghouse, Procter and Gamble, General Electric, General Motors, and hundreds of others, began to introduce their own versions of "Japanese" QWL. Pressure in this direction was further reinforced when Japanese companies such as Nissan, Mitsubishi, Subaru, Toyota, Mazda, Isuzu, and Honda began to build production facilities in Canada and the United States which featured this kind of industrial relations.

So popular has this model become that today QWL programs can be found throughout companies in North America. QWL has become the new buzzword of "progressive" management, and almost overnight we have been flooded with a popular business literature praising QWL, with business school curricula devoting whole courses to analyzing it, and with management consultants referring to it as the soul of modern "corporate culture," as the centerpiece of their personal "philosophy" and "style," as the mysterious key to almost any firm's "pursuit of excellence." Many of the management controls that were intended to make workers think like managers in the 1920s and 1930s have been recycled today. The traditional authoritarian controls remain in place, but they have been disguised and augmented as up-to-date supervisors have attempted to translate the unyielding structures of power into the pop psychology of modern managerialism.

7

Union
Counter-Strategies

Management's renewed enthusiasm for a softer approach to workplace control comes at a time when employers are telling workers and union leaders that if they do not make enormous concessions, they will lose not only their pay and fringe benefits but also their jobs and their unions. At stake in these concessions are most of the gains that labor has made since the 1930s.

Management demands are enormous, both on the job and at the bargaining table. Supervisors are pressuring workers to speed up and then to speed up again. Workers are being forced to cooperate with technological innovations that eliminate their jobs or compel them to work even harder. They are being told to skip breaks, waive safety protections, work compulsory overtime, and surrender a host of things, large and small, that make it possible for people to cope with their jobs. At the negotiating table, unions are being told to forgo wage increases and to accept wage rollbacks. Many employers are also demanding the elimination or reduction of pensions, health care plans, and other benefits.

A large number of formerly powerful unions in steel, transportation, auto, communications, meat packing, construction, warehousing, and other industries have made these concessions, only to find that management then makes further demands—that the grievance procedure be gutted, for example, that union representation in the office and on the shop floor be reduced, that seniority protections be weakened or eliminated, that more jobs be transferred or eliminated.

In industry after industry, management is forcing unions to abandon their master contracts, the very foundation of solidarity between locals, and to replace these industrywide agreements with local "productivity" agreements. Management demands have also been responsible for a flood of two-tier contracts in which new workers receive a fraction of the wages and benefits paid to more senior workers doing the same jobs. Unions that are bound by such contracts (in the mining, aerospace, trucking, auto, electronics, and other industries) have in effect condemned the next generation of members to second-class citizenship and thereby divided their organizations from within. They have also reinforced the popular image of unions as bastions of privilege. The 1980s have also seen a massive increase in the subcontracting of union work to nonunion firms and in "out-sourcing" (importing) of nonunion parts and products into unionized workplaces.

Most unionists who agree to such concessions understand that these changes strike at the heart of what it means to be a union. Nevertheless, they believe that they are faced with a Hobson's choice between their jobs and their unions, and they believe that the health of their unions is the price that must be paid to save what can be saved. Despite the high costs of these concessions, however, workers have been finding that their jobs have not been saved, as layoff after layoff and shutdown after shutdown continues. Their employers have replaced them with robots and computers; they have abandoned them and run away to nonunion, low-wage areas. Many have transferred their operations to third world countries, where wages are less than $2.00 an hour, where abysmal working conditions are the norm, and where genuine unions are systematically suppressed by the local authorities.

Governments in North America have assisted this management offensive by doing little or nothing to stop it. In contrast to countries such as Germany, Belgium, Sweden, Norway, and France, there is no legislation in either Canada or the United States that regulates corporate runaways. More generally, governments have aided management by allowing unemployment levels in both countries to reach post-Depression highs. Unemployment, and the fear of unemployment, have served to keep workers down, both on the job and at the bargaining table. This official tolerance of high unemployment (disguised as fighting inflation, maintaining business confidence, enhancing national economic competitiveness, or cutting the deficit) has been the single most powerful mainstay of the overall attack on labor.

Governments have not been content to be indirect in their support of the corporations. They have also attacked labor directly. Over the past decade in the United States, conservative political allies of business have shattered the once powerful liberal-labor coalitions, defeated progressive changes in labor law (most notably the AFL–CIO-sponsored Labor Law Reform Bill of 1978), and undermined or effectively removed core legislative protections, including the enforcement of workplace health and safety rules, the right to organize, and the right to strike. In state after state, "right-to-work" laws have been enacted in order to deny basic union security measures such as the closed shop (which obliges employers to hire union members) and the union shop (which obliges new employees to join the union). At the same time, the National Labor Relations Board (NLRB) has, among other anti-union rulings, made it easier for unionized companies to shift production to nonunion facilities, and the chairman of the NLRB has declared that "collective bargaining frequently means the destruction of individual freedom and the destruction of the marketplace." Meanwhile, the courts have sided with employers who claim poverty in order to break union contracts. It is in this kind of ideological climate that labor strongholds in the airlines, communications, railroads, and the trucking industry have been deregulated and that jobs in the public sector have been auctioned off to the lowest private-sector bidders.

Although the New Right is not as much in the ascendant in Canada as in the United States, for the past decade the Canadian government has also been indulging in systematic union bashing. This attack has been so broad and so fundamental that Canada has become the only country other than Poland to undergo an on-site investigation by the International Labor Organization into the violation of basic union rights.

The most serious restriction on free collective bargaining has been in the area of back-to-work legislation, whereby the government has removed the right to strike from workers who are exercising their legal right. There have been forty instances of this in the last decade, and in 1982 the basic rights of over 1 million public-sector unionists were suspended in this way. Other Canadian workers have had their right to strike removed through government "designation," according to which the performance of their jobs is deemed necessary to the public interest. In this way, the federal government has removed the right to strike of upward of 40 percent of its union employees. In addition, the courts have become increasingly prone to hand out antipicketing injunctions during legal strikes. Governments at both the national and provincial level in Canada have also enacted wage-control policies that have barred unions from bargaining for wages and benefits above fixed levels. And governments are "privatizing" large chunks of the considerable Canadian public sector, as well as contracting out the jobs of unionized public-sector employees to private nonunion firms.

In tandem with the hard line that employers are pursuing, policies such as these have pushed a great many workers in Canada and the United States out of better-paying jobs with union protection into jobs at or close to the minimum wage in nonunion workplaces. The standard of living of many, especially blue-collar workers, has been declining and indebtedness increasing. There is widespread hidden unemployment: uncalculated numbers of "discouraged" job seekers have given up looking for work, and as many as one in every five workers can find only part-time work. Often even these low-paying and part-time jobs are insecure, and many workers teeter on the unemployment tightrope.

At the same time, governments have been cutting the safety nets out from under those who cannot find work. In Canada, and more aggressively in the United States, governments have been dismantling the very welfare-state programs that unions in particular worked to achieve so that "never again" would the unemployed suffer as they did in the 1930s. Witness the current cutbacks, both actual and threatened, in everything from unemployment insurance to public housing, from medical care to welfare. Witness, too, the growing numbers sleeping "rough" in the public parks and in the bus and subway stations, the lengthening lines outside church soup kitchens, and the crowds at community used-clothing exchanges.

Unemployment, and the fear of unemployment, together with political attacks and the employers' offensive, have put labor on the defensive since the mid-1970s. The strike, conventionally labor's one major weapon, has been on the decline, in both Canada and the United States. Workers who have gone out on strike have had to stay out longer to reach a settlement. Many, such as the strikers at Greyhound and Continental Airlines, for example, or the meatpackers at Gainers in Alberta, have been faced with the most hostile employer intransigence that unionists have had to face in over fifty years. Strike or no strike, many contracts have not kept up with the cost of living, and real wages for many workers are lower now than they were in the early 1970s. Benefits in all areas, but especially in cost-of-living protection, pensions, and paid time off (holidays, vacations, sick leave, bereavement time, etc.) have also been rolled back.

A great many unions, especially in construction and mass production industries in the United States, have lost large portions of their memberships. Some have already been destroyed and more are facing the same fate. It is currently estimated that 28 percent of all nonunion employees in the United States are former union members. So shrunken is the labor movement that now less that 18 percent of all civilian workers in the United States are union members. That is about half the level of unionization of the mid-1950s. Since the 1970s, the unions that were the heart of the union drives of the 1930s— the Steelworkers, Rubber Workers, Auto Workers, and Electrical Workers—have lost at least a third, and in some cases more than half, of their members.

Those losses are not being replaced. Partly because corporations are paying out an estimated $100 million a year to "preventive labor relations" professionals (unionbusters), who use QWL strategies to keep out unions, partly because labor law is so biased and delay-ridden, and partly because pro-union workers are so vulnerable to management reprisals, the rate at which unions are organizing new members today is only a fraction of the pre-1980 levels. Of those few union drives that reach the stage of representation elections, the unions win only about 45 percent compared with a 75 percent win rate in the 1950s.

The few workers who do manage to organize themselves into unions these days are less often the meatpackers and garment workers, the electrical and steel and auto workers, the miners and truckers and the other blue-collar workers who have until recently formed the backbone of militancy and solidarity in the labor movement. Instead, most of the new unionists are coming from among white-collar professional and technical workers in the service, retail, and finance sectors. Because public-sector and other unions with significant white-collar memberships, such as the American Federation of State, County, and Municipal Employees and the Service Employees International Union have been better able to hold onto or increase their numbers, they comprise a growing portion of the labor movement. There is a widespread concern within organized labor that this change in composition may prove to be as much a source of weakness to organized labor as the numerical decline itself. In part, this concern reflects a sexist prejudice against the large number of female white-collar workers coming into the labor movement, but it also reflects a recognition that an increasing proportion of organized labor is made up of unions that are hemmed in by special legal restrictions (public-sector unions) and of unions where the organization of work and other factors have reinforced the members' individualism and inhibited the development of their collective consciousness.

In Canada, the labor movement is stronger in some important respects and union membership remains at about 38 percent of the nonagricultural workforce—twice the U.S. level. Furthermore, the Canadian labor movement is neither as politically isolated nor as unpopular with the public as its counterpart south of the border. At the same time, however, these strengths are offset by serious weaknesses. As in the United States, formerly powerful unions in the manufacturing and resource sectors have been reduced to a fraction of their former dues payers and can no longer lead the labor movement with the same confidence. Due to poor economic conditions, legislative bias, and aggressive encroachments by nonunion contractors, unions in the construction sector have also declined. As in the United States, many of the public-sector unions, now numerically preponderant in the Canadian labor movement, are internally weak, often thanks in no small measure to the government legislation that gave them birth—legislation that built in serious structural divisions and collective-bargaining constraints. For these and other reasons, it is not uncommon for some of the largest public-sector unions to contain locals without functioning steward bodies. Nor is it uncommon for public-sector rank-and-file members to be apathetic, if not openly hostile, to their unions. The Canadian labor movement is also weakened by growing conflicts between its various parts, including tensions between public- and private-sector unions, and divisions between construction unions and the Canadian Labour Congress, Canada's central labor body. For all these reasons, therefore, the Canadian labor movement's greater support and healthier tally of dues-paying members hides an important reality: like its U.S. counterpart, the Canadian labor movement is weaker now than at any time since the 1930s.

It is not by chance that employers and governments extend the olive branch of QWL to labor precisely when they are carrying out a triumphant policy of economic and political aggression. QWL is the other side of this attack, the proverbial velvet glove, the carrot, the honey. The soft sell of QWL goes hand-in-hand with the hard approach. Like the classic squeeze play the police sometimes use during interrogations, the tough cop attacks directly while his partner plays Mr. Nice Guy. Together—the one with the baton and the threats, the other with the concerned look and the sympathetic words—they have a greater chance of getting the cooperation they want. So do employers and politicians. The new industrial relations, combined with this head-on attack, constitute an attempt to put an end to genuine trade unions and the kind of collective bargaining that has been a legitimate part of society in Canada and the United States since before World War II. It is this combination of hard and soft approaches, and the profound challenge it presents to the future of organized labor, that needs to be taken into account when workers and labor leaders devise their own strategies for dealing with QWL.

Despite the fact that QWL programs have been spreading rapidly throughout North America, most unions do not have a coherent policy to deal with their challenges and union leaders are often left to respond on their own. The evaluations of QWL provided in the two case studies, in addition to this analysis of the pattern of soft and hard attacks on the labor movement as a whole, are intended to help such unionists develop counter-strategies specifically tailored to their own needs. *Delays in creating these counter-strategies can make the difference between success and failure.* It is much easier for unionists to have an impact on QWL before it gathers momentum, and far harder to respond to QWL once it is in place, because by then management will have the initiative and the union will, of necessity, be merely reacting. If the union opts to oppose QWL once the program is already underway, its members will be more inclined to see the union's role as one of interference with QWL's promises of progress. Conversely, where the union supports management's QWL initiative, it will likely be seen as an inconsequential "yes person," tagging along behind. The following suggestions are designed to help unionists avoid the pitfalls of delay as well as other dangers.

You will recall that in both case studies there was a major difference between the scope and nature of the initial, more specific QWL program and the program that actually evolved, which became part of a broader, more complex process. Unionists need to appreciate the ways in which QWL initiatives that are explicit and limited may spill over the other—perhaps unforeseen—areas of labor-management relations. They must recognize that management may be letting them in on only part of its plans, permitting the rest to unfold according to a hidden agenda. *In most instances, therefore, unionists will benefit from regarding QWL proposals as part of a broader management strategy.*

Management's ultimate goal, of course, is increased profitability, but unions need to know management's more restricted aims. Is management after a particular department? Is it primarily concerned about more flexibility in assigning jobs? Is it paving the way for the introduction of major technological change? Is QWL and its "beat the competition" message tied to management's demands for collective-bargaining concessions? Improved public relations is frequently another goal. Government agencies in the public eye, or firms concerned about their "poor corporate image," may want to use the progressive aura of QWL for self-advertisement. Timing is likely to be a critical factor: how quickly does management need to achieve these goals? (The degree of the employer's financial difficulties may offer a clue to the projected timetable: all other things being equal, the tighter the profit or budget squeeze, the greater the pressure will be for quick results). Knowing which of these (and other) goals management is after can be the first step in figuring out the game plan for QWL.

Unionists must also come to terms with the broader promises of QWL. This means distinguishing between stated ideals and probable reality. It means answering this question: Is it realistic to expect QWL to contribute to an increase in the workers' power in the workplace and hence improve their work life? These case studies show that QWL has not led to increased in workers' power; quite the reverse. It was used as a management strategy to implement several subtle control mechanisms over workers and their work, and in each case these must be considered and, where they exist, identified.

The next step is to get some sense of how effective these controls are likely to be. What impact are they likely to have on job satisfaction? On solidarity? On the union? On collective bargaining? Of course, the impact of QWL on the workers' relationship to their jobs, to each other, and to management will vary from case to case. What must always be borne in mind is that the intention of QWL-oriented management is to reduce the power of workers, to undermine their solidarity, and to prevent them from aggressively pursuing their own interests.

In many cases, changes in job design will lead to the greatest improvement in job satisfaction. For example, in some QWL "greenfield" sites (where completely new production facilities are being built and a new work force is being recruited), unionists may be called on to cooperate with management in "socio-technical" job designs. According to the textbooks, such job design techniques are meant to develop the best fit between the technical requirements of production and the social and psychological needs of workers. To the extent that this theory holds true, such job design processes may lead to fundamental change, although the requirements of the "technical" will normally outweigh the needs of the "socio"—that is, management's production goals will shape the kind of adjustments required of the "human factor."

In already existing workplaces, however, the most fundamental job redesign that is likely to be achieved is what is loosely termed "job enrichment," which means a qualitative upgrading of job skills and/or responsibilities. An example would be the boosters' jobs in the auto plant. This is also the kind of job redesign that is most likely to involve a shift in authority from front-line supervisors to selected line workers. As we have seen, this kind of job redesign may well lead to an increase in job satisfaction because it gives the workers additional influence over their jobs. At the same time, it is important to recognize that this margin of influence may well apply to relatively few workers (perhaps at the expense of other, more skilled workers), that it is confined by the overall limits of management control, and that it makes these workers into agents of that control as they come to think of themselves as "foremen without ties." Workers will often have more *real* power in the workplace through bolstering their solidarity with each other and through their ability to resist rather than through their collaboration with management.

Less profound changes in job design are often called by such terms as "job enlargement" (the combination of several similar jobs into one larger one) and "job rotation." Here there is no qualitative change in the content of the job, however, and the impact on job satisfaction is not likely to be major or long-lasting. In Trim in the car plant, for example, many workers appreciated the opportunity to learn new jobs but very few actually wanted to rotate jobs on a regular basis. Having to do several bad jobs is often considered worse than just doing one.

Whatever the objective changes, the impact of QWL on worker solidarity will depend a great deal on how much change there is in the workers' attitudes toward their jobs. The loss of solidarity that results when management is able to harness work groups to its profit goals has already been stressed. Another issue is the impact of the rate and pattern of diffusion of QWL. Where the timing and the extent of diffusion are slow and uneven across the workplace, the diffusion process itself is liable to become a center of tension and conflict among the workers. As has also been stressed, the isolation of, and competition between, work groups has the greatest potential for harming worker solidarity, as does productivity and job competition between locals in the same union.

Experienced unionists will be the first to recognize that the impact of QWL will be highly dependent on outside economic factors. Right now, hard times are the most important suppressor of solidarity and of workers' willingness to resist management aggression. Hard times also encourage workers to believe that QWL will save their jobs (unless the economic outlook is so bad that it shatters the basis of that hope, as happened at the electronics plant). A certain amount of fear, combined with vague promises of a more pleasant style of supervision and work, can be exceedingly persuasive. As has been shown, QWL and hard times reinforce each other, the soft line and the hard line. Unionists caught in the middle may find the pressures and temptations hard to resist.

Whatever the conditions, QWL will have serious implications for union leadership and organization. As the case studies show, the challenge of QWL to the labor movement is enormous. In developing their response, unionists will need to consider three needs in particular: first, the need to respond to the positive image painted of QWL by its proponents; second, the need to promote unity in the union leadership; and third, the absolutely critical need to develop healthier and stronger ties between a union's leaders and its members. All of these needs deserve serious attention, irrespective of the other aspects of union policy and practice regarding QWL.

The first need is related to the fact that QWL can have an enormous public relations value for governments and corporations which foster them. There are several dimensions to this, but one that is of special concern to unionists is the implication that hard times—our high unemployment, our export problems, our increasing government deficits—are largely due to wages being too high and workers being too lazy or too militant. Such myths are widely believed and underlie the popular penchant for scapegoating workers and their unions. QWL can make this knee-jerk reflex to blame the victim even worse because it places unionists in a peculiar bind: support of QWL may be seen as a tacit admission that this is indeed a nation of bum workers (especially unionized bum workers), while opposition to QWL may be seen as evidence that reactionary labor bosses and their dupes are afraid of progress. The name alone—

quality of working life—is so smooth and pleasant that unionists who turn down this apparent nirvana can be portrayed as insane—or arrogant, cruel, ignorant, and smug about the serious problems that people face at work.

To get out of this bind, unionists need to respond with their own public relations campaign. One way to do this is to take the promises of QWL at face value and pursue the logic of management's stated concern to improve the lives of the workers. In a recent discussion paper, "Towards a Trade Union QWL Agenda," the Canadian office of the United Steelworkers reminded its readers that unions have been trying to improve the quality of working life for a very long time—through collective bargaining. The Steelworkers stress that there are many issues affecting the quality of working life, including "joint administration of insurance and pension funds, justice and dignity, sexual harassment, maternity leaves with pay, child care, technological change, incentive pay, etc. which managements presently are reluctant to deal with." The Steelworkers continue: "If quality of working life is a government policy aimed at society at large, then removal of the impediments to union organization should be reflected in amendments to the labour law."

Responses such as these go a long way toward placing the onus for improving the quality of working life where it should be—on those with the real power to do something about it. In reply, governments and private employers may argue that these issues are not, technically speaking, QWL. Precisely—and so much for the attempt to blame workers and unions for their lack of cooperation in the workplace.

Regardless of the rhetoric surrounding QWL, fundamental conflicts of interest between management and labor emerge sooner or later: QWL or no QWL, management will eventually push to speed up work, lower wages and benefits, contract out jobs, employ labor-displacing technology, and demand a host of other concessions. In many cases, too, employers are introducing QWL as part of a two-pronged strategy: they are using QWL as a means of obtaining cooperation in union workplaces while they expand production to nonunion operations. None of this is a matter of "immoral" or "irresponsible" or "heartless" employers; it is simply the nature of the "bottom line" of profit in market economies. It is this intractable conflict at the heart of the relationship between employers and workers which makes meaningful cooperation between the two so impossibly one-sided. By effectively exposing this truth, unionists can go a long way toward warding off the effects of the employers' QWL-inspired public relations campaigns against workers and unions.

The second key challenge is the need to counter any tendency to undermine the unity of the union leadership. This tendency stems from a premise that lies at the heart of QWL, namely, that there are major areas, separate and distinct from other areas of labor-management conflict, where both sides can make big gains from cooperation. As has already been shown, this premise is naive at best and dangerous in its implications for unions. The attempt to separate "win-win" from "win-lose" areas can easily lead to divisions in the union leadership. Individual leaders are asked to play Dr. Jekyll one minute and Mr. Hyde the next, or one level of the leadership is expected to specialize in the adversarial role while another level plays the cooperative role. This kind of acting can lead to a great deal of confusion (if not to real schizophrenia).

In countries such as Norway and Sweden, and to a lesser extent in Germany, unions have been able to separate areas of conflict from areas of cooperation without doing intolerable damage to unity within the union leadership (although even in these countries unions have had serious problems with this), in part because political and economic conditions there are quite different from those in the United States and Canada. In such countries, a very large proportion of workers belong to unions (in Sweden and Norway the vast majority are organized). In addition, unions tend to be highly centralized and enjoy strong protective legislation, brought in by the social democratic governments that have been in power throughout most of the postwar period. In the United States and Canada, by contrast, none of these conditions prevail. Governments have generally been more conservative in both countries, and especially so in the United States. Although the New Democratic Party (NDP) espouses a social democratic platform during Canadian elections and has formed governments in three western provinces, it has far less clout than its counterparts in Europe and has never formed a national government. Moreover, as a general rule, the closer the NDP has been to power, the further it has distanced itself from the primary interests of the labor movement. The situation in the United States is worse, of course: a social democratic party is not even part of the Congressional system.

Furthermore, as in the United States, labor unions in Canada are far weaker than they are in Europe, and the Canadian labor movement is highly balkanized by regionalism and by the fact that labor legislation is primarily a provincial jurisdiction. Although labor legislation in the United States is mainly a federal matter, there are enormous regional differences in the U.S. labor movement as well, and, as indicated earlier, the overall situation faced by organized labor is even worse. Moreover, in both countries it is common for collective bargaining to focus on the local union level, so that any attempt to play the roles of adversary and cooperator at the same time is extremely difficult, and the chances that such an attempt will lead to increased tension, confusion, and disunity within the local leadership are far greater.

Certainly this was the experience of the union leaders at Progress Motors, and the result was a bitterly divided local leadership. The lesson to be learned here is that unionists need to be wary of becoming involved in top-down QWL schemes. Local leaders who make policy decisions regarding QWL on their own risk ending up on their own—particularly when management does not deliver on the promises that are used to sell QWL. Unionists who think they are cunning enough to please both their members and management may end up being too clever by half.

Meeting this threat to leadership unity requires a vigorous, union-controlled educational campaign, if possible *before management initiates QWL*. In most cases this campaign should start with the needs and concerns of the stewards and other local leaders. It should deal frankly with the ways management can use QWL to exploit their political weaknesses, both in relation to each other and in relation to those they represent. Beyond this, *it is imperative for unions to educate all their members about QWL and, again, it is best to do this before management does.*

If this education campaign is to succeed, union leaders and "rank and file" workers will need to participate in their own education, to go beyond the passive absorption of knowledge that educators all too often impose. This education will have to focus on encouraging those who are learning about QWL to become an integral part of an activist strategy for personally *doing* something about it. Those who are being educated will need to examine QWL from many different perspectives, not just those that are favored by their educators. And they will need to identify clear *collective* goals for improving their working lives—a *union* agenda for achieving goals such as better workplace health and safety, genuine job security, gender and racial equality in hiring, training, and promotion practices, more time off the job for union activities, more realistic workloads, and so on.

Since QWL is an ongoing process, this education campaign will have to be ongoing as well. To this end, it may be worthwhile to set up local, regional, and national union committees to investigate QWL as it spreads and evolves, to keep union leaders and members informed about its development, to do surveys of the responses and needs of members in regard to QWL, and to contribute in other ways to their continuing education about it. Such an educational campaign should reduce or eliminate the need to rely on outside QWL consultants, most of whom are likely to know a great deal less about the specific needs and objectives of the union than those unionists who are involved in the campaign. Where outside QWL consultants are still necessary, it is preferable for the union to have full control over their selection, funding, and job description, and the timing of the termination of their contracts. It is also important to bear in mind that there is more at issue than whether the consultants are sympathetic to labor: no matter what their attitude, the consultants will be committed to QWL— and it is QWL itself, through its control by management, that is not neutral.

The third need that deserves serious attention is to develop ways to cement the ties between the local leaders and the members. *In the longer run, this is the most crucial task of all.* As the case studies show, QWL reduces what workers have in common in the workplace by turning collective interests into individual ones. This may come about through job redesign or through informal accommodations between supervisors and workers. Even minor, short-term benefits to favored workers are liable to make for increased individualism and further enhance unevenness of conditions across the marketplace. It is this unevenness of treatment and conditions that makes it more difficult for union leaders to articulate the common needs of workers and to respond to those needs in ways that are fair and equal across the membership.

There are two general ways to strengthen workers' ties to their union. The first involves reaching out to get more of the membership to play an active role in the union. The second involves incorporating more of the promised benefits of QWL into the collective bargaining process. Either or both tacks can be taken.

In the first place, an attempt can be made to bring more rank-and-file workers into the process of creating the union's strategy for dealing with QWL. For instance, the local QWL education and investigation committees (mentioned above) can be opened up to new membership. Unionists may also want to consider broadening the formal leadership of the union. Depending on the prevailing circumstances, this can be achieved, for example, by increasing the number of stewards, by creating assistant stewards, by rotating stewards, and in some cases by limiting the number of terms of office a steward may serve. Where warranted, these kinds of reforms can be extended to other union offices as well.

To further stimulate the members' involvement, unionists

may decide to push for a decentralization of *selected* aspects of the collective bargaining process to a local level, extending "local issue" bargaining and making it a more significant part of contract talks. It may also be possible, and desirable, that bargaining around some issues involving working conditions be made ongoing rather than periodic, in the same way that health-and-safety committees are ongoing in many workplaces. In addition to exciting greater member attention, such bargaining may enable unionists to gain benefits for the entire membership that would otherwise have been made available to only a few members. This can help to make issues more common to all the members, so that tendencies promoting envy and discord among those workers who are being treated differently are reduced. *Properly coordinated,* such a selective decentralization of collective bargaining can enable the union to respond more quickly, specifically, and effectively to QWL initiatives. Under certain circumstances, it can allow the union itself to take the initiative. This is especially important where management uses QWL-inspired variations in pay, jobs, and working conditions among different workplaces as a basis for running back and forth between locals in a permanent quest for ever more concessions. Union leaders can help to turn these same variations to their advantage by choosing the best features in each workplace to create a standard set of goals—a *union* quality of working life agenda—for all the locals in the union. Common positive objectives can help to reduce the feelings of powerlessness and separateness in various workplaces that provide open invitations for employers to divide unions from within.

The second general way to strengthen workers' ties to their unions, which can be pursued either as an alternative to the first or in conjunction with it, involves bringing the promises of QWL into the formal collective bargaining process. This can help to ensure that any benefits are made as general as possible, giving management less chance to play favorites or set worker against worker. In addition, when these changes are incorporated into formal contract language, they become legally binding. Since issues concerning working conditions often involve what have long been considered management's rights, this elevation of QWL issues into the collective bargaining process also implies a potential broadening of the range of legitimate worker control in the workplace.

A case in point is the "justice-and-dignity" clause that the Steelworkers have succeeded in incorporating into the agreement covering the can industry in North America. This clause places an important limit on management's right to discipline workers by giving the workers what should be an elementary right—to be considered innocent until proven guilty. This is the reverse of the standard procedure, where workers are judged guilty and penalized until their innocence is established. Under the new contract clause, workers have the right to stay on the job with pay until an arbitrator rules on the case or some other resolution occurs.

Even where there is little likelihood that such gains can be made in contract talks, unionists may wish to push for them. This is especially important if management decides to hand out, on an informal and piecemeal basis, what it denies through collective bargaining. This kind of employer tactic can undermine the legitimacy of the union in the eyes of the membership. Where feasible, unionists may want to go on the offensive and publicize what management is doing to the membership. Where the benefits management has handed out to favored workers or work groups would be worthwhile for the membership generally, the union can point out management's manipulative intent and demand that management provide the benefits to everyone.

Hypocritical employers can be pressured in other ways. If they claim to be committed to QWL and state that from now on the workers are to be trusted and treated like human beings, it may be worthwhile demanding concessions that are consistent with these claims—job security guarantees, guarantees against speedup, the elimination of punch clocks, access to company books, and a whole list of assurances of good faith. Where management concedes some of these claims, the concessions will be shown to be in response to the collective efforts of the workers and their union. Even where management is only willing to make informal agreements rather than binding ones, unionists may find it to their advantage to publish these concessions so that the costs of reneging will be more damaging. When management refuses to make good on its promises of more humane treatment, the hypocrisy will be exposed for all to see.

QWL-encouraged job competition between workers, between locals, and between unions is another way to divide unions from within. In order to ward off pressures on workers in different parts of the same industry or company to engage in this type of competition, unionists need to strengthen the kind of industrywide pattern bargaining which minimizes the differences in wages and work rules between companies. Unionists also need to strengthen the horizontal links between locals. Shared educational programs about the pitfalls of QWL and shared strategy planning, for example, can strengthen solidarity at this level. This is particularly crucial during a management offensive aimed at dismantling industrywide agreements through local productivity bargaining.

These are the kinds of practical initiatives unionists can take in order to fight this type of management control at the local level. Unionists must also realize, however, that QWL is part of a much broader offensive on the part of corporations and governments. Unions in the United States and Canada, as well as throughout most of the Western world, are facing the most concerted attack in postwar history. The objective of this offensive is nothing less than an end to trade unionism as we know it. So far it has been successful. As has been argued, labor is paying the costs of the continuing recession in many different ways: millions of unemployed, declining real wages, increasing and more regressive taxes, mounting management aggression in the workplace, restricted access to unemployment insurance, a critical lack of affordable housing, the withdrawal of a wide range of public services—the fronts in the attack on the workers' standard of living are almost endless. The result is the shattering of individual lives, of families, of communities.

The modern labor movement has faced other offensives throughout its history, but there has never been an onslaught quite like this one. The difference is in part in its magnitude, but it is also that labor's enemies talk of peace as they carry on war. Workers hear politicians talking benignly, if vaguely, of "fairness," of plans for "worker ownership," of schemes for labor to become a "full partner in the process of economic recovery," of intentions to give labor "an equal voice in the resolution of issues like technological change and productivity improvement." Respected union leaders are called on to sit down with business leaders on QWL advisory boards. They are being asked to join the boards of the very corporations they are fighting. In Canada, they have even been asked to work with business and government to set up a multi-million-dollar "thinktank" to solve the economic crisis. They have been invited to sit down with the federal government to advise on more cutbacks in social programs. One of the reasons QWL is so seductive is that it is strongly promoted by politicians who are considered friends of labor. In Canada, there are prominent QWL advocates within the New Democratic Party, the party with the strongest ties to organized labor. In the United States, support for QWL is far more often found within the Democratic Party (especially its liberal and labor wing) than in the Republican Party. Whereas the right has historically been more direct and draconian in its labor relations policies, it is frequently the left of the political mainstream in both Canada and the United States that has appealed to voters on the need for softer approaches, in the name of national competitiveness and a renewed social unity.

At the same time that politicians and employers are calling for a new spirit of "harmony" in the workplace, workers are being pressured to make a wide range of concessions and the most massive surge of technological change in the modern era is sweeping away whole occupations and even entire industries. While the mass media report growing public hostility toward labor unions, they ignore management's daily aggression on the job and blame workers for the corporations' failure to win the international productivity race. Yet so high are the costs in human misery that this is a race very few would actually want to win, much less compete in: consider the sacrifices it would take to be wage-competitive with the near-slave-labor conditions in much of the third world. In Brazil the average hourly wage is $1.68. In Korea it is $1.29. In Taiwan it is $1.61. Does anyone seriously believe that Canadians and Americans should aspire to a standard of living that is a mere one-tenth of the current standard? While many productive workers stagger under a heavier economic burden, corporate offices have become bloated with executives "earning" six- and seven-figure salaries. "Free" enterprise gorges on tax write-offs, "forgivable" loans, and a myriad of other direct and indirect donations from the public treasury. The recipients of this public generosity are the very people who are so fond of telling workers that there is no such thing as a free lunch.

All this is going on while QWL consultants exhort workers to step right up for a "good job," a "secure job," a job where they will find "enjoyment, accomplishment, and pride," where they will have "optimal variety" as well as "challenge and ongoing opportunities to learn." They tell workers about "democratic principles," the "joint control and shared responsibility between union and management at all levels," and they speak about the "right to have some say over all things that affect you."

In one sense, there is nothing wrong with this kind of sales pitch: it reminds workers of what they need and have a right to aim for, and it may contribute to the kind of broader social and political orientation that will help the labor movement break out of the ideological and practical confines of apolitical business unionism. At the same time, as the events at Progress Motors and Universal Electric so clearly show, workers and unions are faced with an immediate, fundamental fact: *management controls QWL*. While management's style of control may change, there is no real change in management's "right" to control production. Because of this, and because management enjoys the backing of most of the other major power centers in society, employers win and workers lose. Despite the image of "Big Labor" as one of a triumvirate of equals with "Big Business" and "Big Government," labor never sits down at their table as an equal. This is just as true whether the table is for a QWL steering committee or a collective-bargaining session.

Today, this imbalance of power between workers and bosses is deteriorating further, and there is no doubt that the labor movement is in the midst of a crisis of survival. At the same time, this crisis presents the labor movement with a historic opportunity. Workers and their unions have an enormous potential advantage: the power of numbers. Labor's potential power lies not only in its own numbers but in those of its emerging allies in the women's movement, the peace movement, the ecology movement, farm organizations, and organizations of nonwhite groups. Labor is developing further alliances with many of the church and community groups that are organizing the growing numbers of the homeless, sick, elderly, unemployed, and poor. Like workers, these people have also been victims of the offensive by employers and governments. Desperation is not enough, of course, and to win these numbers will need to be united and mobilized behind a common coalition strategy that is capable of moving beyond opposition to create concrete political alternatives. This coalition will need not only to work toward a common vision of a better society, but to take full account of the complex diversity and fluid boundaries within its own constituent organizations. Across Canada and the United States such broad-based coalitions are already building.

Thus far, however, organized labor has been among the least prepared to mobilize its own numbers. Effective mobilization will require a major commitment and effort by grassroots unionists to educate themselves about the gravity of the offensive that the employers and governments are conducting. Unionists will need to become active in shaping the emerging alternatives. This will mean turning away from QWL's dangerous ideological premise that what is good for business is good for labor. Instead of the "cooperation" being promoted by politicians and employers, it will mean developing the collective power to bring about more enduring and beneficial, more democratic and genuine, kinds of cooperation to fulfill the empty promises of QWL.

Further Reading

There are thousands of books, pamphlets, and articles about Quality of Working Life programs, and more are being written every day. However, from labor's perspective much of this material is useless. Lacking adequate factual basis, authors often fail to move beyond vague generalities. Those who pay attention to concrete workplace realities frequently ignore or gloss over those concerns that are most relevant to workers and unions: the impact of QWL on job satisfaction, worker solidarity, collective bargaining, the grievance procedure, relations between workers and supervisors, and relations between union leaders and the "rank and file."

Reasons for these deficiencies are not hard to find. Much of what has been written about QWL has come from professional consultants or academics who are paid by management to promote and set up QWL programs. Very few of these consultants and academics have personal experience as workers or trade unionists, and those who have been directly involved in production relations have more often than not been members of management. Added to the biases of self-interest and management roles are biases stemming from intellectual conditioning: many of those who write about QWL have a preoccupation with individual and small-group psychology—a preoccupation that has frequently been detrimental to an appreciation of fundamental relations of power in the workplace. Finally, much of the quality of the literature reflects a largely uncritical popular interest in management "style" and in particular a superficial fascination with Japanese management practices centered on small groups. As a consequence of these factors, much of the burgeoning literature about QWL is intellectually shoddy; it is at best naive, over-general, and irrelevant, at worst self-serving and intentionally propagandistic.

Fortunately, there are a number of exceptions. Following are some books and articles, most of which are written from a labor perspective, that stand out as thoughtful contributions to an understanding of this new wave of "work humanization." They will be of special interest to the reader who wishes to know more about the impact of QWL programs on workers and unions.

Asplund, Christer. *Redesigning Jobs: Western European Experiences.* Brussels: European Trade Union Institute, 1981.

Asplund presents a clear and comprehensive examination of the responses of Western European trade unions to various forms of QWL. He stresses that even where unions have initiated demands for these workplace reforms, management has fashioned QWL in accordance with its own ends. At the same time, he concludes that since management needs worker involvement in job redesign in order to minimize worker resistance, unions can have some influence in this area, and he provides a list of union stipulations that may be built into the collective-bargaining process around job redesign.

de Boer, Jack. "The Quality of Work Life Strategy and Worker Participation in Decision-Making." M.A. thesis, Environmental Studies Program, York University (Toronto), 1979.

The author argues that QWL should be evaluated less according to its impact on job satisfaction than on its impact on workers' participation in decision-making. He maintains that the failure of most QWL analysts to distinguish between "dependent" and "independent" power has resulted in a widespread confusion over the difference between "felt" power and "real" power in the workplace. He provides a useful and perceptive discussion of the need for greater union control over QWL programs and for increased union power in relation to higher level corporate decision-making.

Dohse, Knuth, Jurgens, Ulrich, and Thomas Malsch. "From 'Fordism' to 'Toyotism'? The Social Organization of the Labor Process in the Japanese Automobile Industry." *Politics and Society* 14, no. 2 (1985).

The authors maintain that the Japanese industrial relations system is made possible by the removal of limits on management power and by the systematic undermining of worker solidarity. They conclude that worker participation "occurs in a controlled context in which the topics, goals, and forms of articulation are, for practical purposes, limited to company interests."

Ellinger, Charles, and Bruce Nissen. "A Case Study of a Failed QWL Program: Implications for Labor Education." *Labour Studies Journal* (Winter 1987).

Evidence from a large manufacturing plant shows that QWL interfered with the union's role in both collective bargaining and the grievance procedure, and that it generated a number of "political problems" for the union leadership. When the union tried to use QWL methods in collective bargaining, the membership rejected the contract because they thought their bargaining committee was "in bed with management." Ellinger and Nissen recommend that instead of being a "cheerleader," educators should explain QWL's "difficulties and dangers" to local unions.

Gryzb, Gerard J. "Decollectivization and Recollectivization in the Workplace: The Impact of Technology on Informal Work Groups and Work Culture." *Economic and Industrial Democracy* (November 1981).

Gryzb argues that management is using new technology to destroy the solidarity of traditional informal work groups and that QWL is being used as a substitute in order to create a work culture that enhances management control.

Heckscher, Charles. "Multilateral Negotiation and the Failure of American Labor." *Negotiations Journal* (April 1986).

Although much of Heckscher's description of the crisis facing organized labor is insightful, his prescription of "associational unionism" is ultimately a call for a new, less obvious form of company unionism. The main significance of the author's provocative argument lies in its appreciation of the implications of QWL for the future of organized labor.

Heckscher, Charles. "Worker Participation and Management Control." *Journal of Social Reconstruction* (January-March 1980).

The author rejects conventional explanations of the roots of worker participation schemes in favor of the view thatt the changing needs of large businesses and the nature of work in the service sector have created new pressures for the organizational integration of workers. He surveys the effectiveness of various forms of QWL, paying special attention to autonomous work groups. Predicting that QWL will help to divide the working class between those in relatively advantaged core firms and those in weaker peripheral firms, he stresses the need for unions to develop "a positive vision of worker participation to set against management's corporatist ideal. . . ."

Hunnius, Gerry. "On the Nature of Capitalist-Initiated Innovations in the Workplace." In *Power and Work: The Liberation of Work and the Control of Political Power,* edited by Tom R. Burns, Lars Erik Karlsson, and Veljko Rus. London: Sage Publications, 1979.

In addition to an excellent critical analysis of the German model of "co-determination" and tendencies toward this form of labor-management cooperation in Canada, Hunnius provides a nuanced appraisal of the similarities and differences between classical "human relations" approaches and contemporary QWL programs.

Junkerman, John. "'We are Driven!' Life on the Fast Line at Datsun." *Mother Jones* (August 1982).

This account of industrial relations at the Nissan Motor Company in Japan describes the role of the Japanese auto workers union as an arm of management control and examines the ways quality control circles promote an intensification of work. Although there is discontent within the Nissan workforce, the author explains that worker resistance is effectively contained by both management and the union.

Katz, Harry C. *Shifting Gears: Changing Labor Relations in the U.S. Automobile Industry.* Boston: M.I.T. Press, 1985.

This study contrasts the labor relations model that emerged in the automobile industry after World War II with the changes that are now taking place. Much of the study focusses on innovations at General Motors plants. Special attention is given to the role that the GM "team system" can play in promoting increased flexibility in job classifications and other work rules. Katz argues that this flexibility is consistent with the capabilities of new technology, with the challenges associated with increased market volatility, and with new pressure to cut costs and improve quality. He further argues that the team system would "change but not diminish the role of the local union."

Kelly, John E. *Scientific Management, Job Re-design, and Work Performance.* New York: Academic Press, 1982.

Kelly provides a critique of the major assumptions underlying classical job redesign theory and argues that management's production and cost problems rather than personnel problems are the main causes of job redesign. He describes how the nature of job redesign varies between mass industry, services, and continuous-flow industries. He concludes that many unions are likely either to stall management attempts to change job structures or else to become closer "partners" with management. Others, however, may be encouraged to make a reappraisal of work and employment along the lines of the "workers' alternative plans" movement in Britain. (On this, see Huw Beynon and Hilary Wainwright, *The Workers' Report on Vickers* [London: Pluto Press, 1979]; Mike Cooley, *Architect or Bee?: The Human/Technology Relationship* [Boston: South End Press, 1982]; and Hilary Wainwright and Dave Elliott, *The Lucas Plan: A New Trade Unionism in the Making?* [London: Allison and Busby, 1982].)

Kelly, John E. "A Reappraisal of Sociotechnical Systems Theory." *Human Relations* (December 1978).

Kelly presents a reinterpretation of those case studies in Britain, India, and Norway that were the principal basis for the theory supporting the "sociotechnical" form of QWL. According to the author, these management innovations promoted the introduction of greater workloads and faster pacing of work. He also concludes that the contribution of pay incentives to improved product quality and increased output was underestimated in the original case studies.

Kochan, Thomas A., Harry C. Katz, and Nancy R. Mower. "Worker Participation and American Unions." In *Challenges and Choices Facing American Labor,* edited by Thomas A. Kochan. Boston: MIT Press, 1985.

This article is based on data from a survey questionnaire conducted in five unionized workplaces with ongoing QWL programs. With some exceptions, the data indicate that QWL was not generally beneficial to the workers and did not increase their influence over job-related issues. The study contains an insightful discussion of the implications of worker-participation schemes on industrial relations and labor law in the United States.

Mann, Eric. "Cooperation for What? U.A.W. Backs the Wrong Team." *The Nation,* 14 February 1987.

Mann maintains that the "team concept" is being sold to auto workers as a way to improve production efficiency but that it is part of a plan to cut jobs. An auto worker himself, he describes how management threatened to shut down his plant in order to gain the workers' consent to implement the team concept, thereby pitting his local in a job competition against another UAW local. Mann believes that this undermined the development of a popular coalition against plant shutdowns. He maintains that this is typical of the current direction of the UAW and proposes key parts of an alternative strategy for rebuilding the union "from the bottom up."

Nichols, Theo, and Huw Beynon. *Living with Capitalism: Class Relations and the Modern Factory.* London: Routledge and Kegan Paul, 1977.

The authors focus on a worker-participation program at a small chemical plant in England. They examine the cooptation of local shop stewards and the training of managers in the appropriate "style" as part of an attempt to turn the trade union into an arm of management control. They also explore the critical contradictions that this approach poses for management, the union, and the workers.

Nichols, Theo. "The 'Socialism' of Management: Some Comments on the New 'Human' Relations." *Sociological Review* (May 1975).

Nichols makes the case that if capital-intensive technologies are to operate continuously with maximum efficiency, management needs an involved and flexible workforce. Job enrichment and worker participation are attempts to solve this "problem of motivation" for management. He warns that such changes are not likely to encourage workers' demands for fundamental changes in power in the workplace.

Noble, David F. *Forces of Production: A Social History of Industrial Automation.* New York: Alfred A Knopf, 1984.

This book includes a detailed description of a QWL experiment to improve worker motivation at a General Electric plant after the introduction of expensive numerical-control technology. Noble draws insightful connections between QWL programs and the enhancement of productivity. He concludes that management is prone to revert to traditional authoritarian controls if QWL is perceived as a threat to its control over the labor process.

Parker, Mike. *Inside the Circle: A Union Guide to QWL.* Boston: South End Press, 1985.

This book contains a comprehensive and balanced critique of the dangers of QWL from a labor perspective. Parker includes a wealth of practical information that is designed to aid the development of union counter-strategies. The sections dealing with the ideological implications of QWL programs are especially interesting. The straightforward writing style, short chapters, and effective use of graphics make this book an excellent tool for trade union education.

Parker, Mike, and Dwight Hanson. "The Circle Game." *The Progressive* (January 1983).

Parker and Hansen provide an inside look at the operation of a QWL program in a Michigan automobile plant and draw causal connections between QWL and concessions-bargaining by the union. Like de Boer (above), they argue for a clear distinction between "participation" and "power" and specify ways that unions can develop an alternative QWL agenda.

Ramsay, Harvie. "Cycles of Control: Worker Participation in Historical Perspective." *Sociology* (September 1977).

The author argues that cycles of worker participation in Britain have arisen during periods when management felt that its power was threatened. He maintains that various management schemes, including the emergence of arbitration and conciliation procedures, profit-sharing, the rise of joint labor-management committees at the level of the firm after World War I, the revival of labor-management consultation after World War II, and the current wave of worker-participation programs are all evidence that "capitalism both engenders and renders impotent such movements. . . ."

Rinehart, James. *The Tyranny of Work: Alienation and the Labor Process*. 2nd ed., Toronto: Harcourt Brace Jovanovich, 1987.

Using a straightforward and concise writing style, Rinehart demonstrates the connections between the earlier human relations approach and contemporary forms of participative management. He offers incisive critiques of various forms of QWL and clearly distinguishes them from the history and forms of genuine workers' control.

Rinehart, James. "Improving the Quality of Working Life Through Job Redesign: Work Humanization or Work Rationalization?" *Canadian Review of Sociology and Anthropology* 23, no. 4 (1986).

Job redesign is less an attempt to pacify workers, says Rinehart, than management's response to new technological and economic conditions that make maximum job simplification unprofitable. Although increased job satisfaction may occur, he argues that this is limited and may be offset by work intensification, job loss, and the undermining of workers' collective capacity to defend their interests.

Rinehart, James. "Appropriating Workers' Knowledge: Quality Control Circles at a General Motors Plant." *Studies in Political Economy* (Spring 1984).

This is a case study of a joint union-management QWL project at a General Motors diesel plant. It contains an excellent evaluation of the way management uses QWL training methods and appeals to a "depression psychology" in order to shape worker consciousness in favor of management goals. The author examines the potential dangers this program posed for the union.

Roberts, Ceridwen, and Stephen Wood. "Collective Bargaining and Job Redesign." In *Autonomy and Control at the Workplace: Contexts for Job Redesign,* edited by John E. Kelly and Chris W. Clegg. London: Croom Helm, 1982.

This article is based on a case study of a "new working relationship agreement" between labor and management at a large unionized firm in Britain. The authors found that, although there were variations among different kinds of workers, job enrichment was of less importance to workers than factors such as pay and job security. Job redesign was less an attempt to "con" workers, they argue, than a desire by management to respond to new economic and technological needs, which required a different kind of supervision and a more flexible workforce. Roberts and Wood stress that management was not wholly successful in satisfying this desire because the workers were able to resist.

Shaiken, Harley, Herzenberg, Stephen, and Sarah Kuhn. "The Work Process Under More Flexible Production." *Industrial Relations* 23, no. 2 (1986).

According to the authors' assessment of case studies covering thirteen industrial work sites, managers are using QWL programs and appeals to an "ideology of competition," in conjunction with technological changes, to increase their control over the work process and to intensify work by "encouraging their employees to internalize the company goals of efficiency and equality."

Thomas, Robert J. "Quality and Quantity? Worker Participation in the U.S. and Japanese Automobile Industries." In *Technological Change and Worker Movements,* edited by Melvin Dubofsky. Beverly Hills: Sage, 1985.

On the basis of his evaluation of two kinds of worker participation schemes (problem-solving groups and employee-management communication programs), Thomas concludes that these schemes increase management control over workers while undermining their capacity to question managerial authority. He also questions the long term viability of Japanese quality control circles and the appropriateness of attempts to transplant such practices to U.S. enterprises.

Wood, Stephen. "Cooperative Labor Strategy in the U.S. Auto Industry." *Economic and Industrial Democracy* 7 (1986).

Wood maintains that QWL programs in auto assembly plants have not been associated with fundamental changes in the organization of work. Instead, they have brought about changes in supervisory style, promoted "cost and quality consciousness" among workers, and encouraged competition between workers in different plants of the same company. He examines the contradictions between improved job security and the auto companies' involvement in overseas operations, joint ventures, the importing of components, etc. QWL is compatible with traditional management controls, he observes, and it is part of a wider management strategy to undermine unions.

Wrenn, Robert. "Management and Work Humanization." *The Insurgent Sociologist* 11, no. 3 (1982).

This article contains a useful survey of a great deal of the relevant literature concerning various elements of QWL. The author also examines the history of key QWL experiments and assesses whether or not these innovations pose a threat to either management control or to capitalism.

Videotapes

Like the literature about QWL, most videotapes on the subject are designed for management-oriented public relations or educational campaigns to promote QWL. The following videotapes, however, provide a more critical, labor-oriented perspective, and are very useful for trade union education.

"QWL: Nothing to Lose But Your Job." Approximately 30 minutes, 1985.

Using film of actual QWL team sessions and management-training exercises, this videotape examines the implications of QWL for workers and trade unions. It is available from the Labor Media Group, P.O. Box 7266, Ann Arbor, MI.

"We Are Driven." Approximately 60 minutes, 1984.

This videotape focuses on the attempt to implement Japanese management practices at a Nissan automobile plant in Smyrna, Tennessee. It is available from WGBH Distribution, 125 Western Avenue, Boston, MA.

Networking

Rank-and-file trade unionists in Canada have formed their own network to keep in touch and share news and views about QWL. The network is called KAIZEN, a Japanese term that (loosely translated) means "work smart." KAIZEN may be contacted through Bruce May and Mac McNair at Suite 400, 105 Carlton Street, Toronto, Ontario, Canada (tel.: 416-977-4261).